Ernest Mason Satow

Kinse Shiriaku

A history of Japan from the first visit of Commodore Perry in 1853 to the capture of

Kakodate by the Mikado's forces in 1869

Ernest Mason Satow

Kinse Shiriaku
A history of Japan from the first visit of Commodore Perry in 1853 to the capture of Kakodate by the Mikado's forces in 1869

ISBN/EAN: 9783337164188

Printed in Europe, USA, Canada, Australia, Japan

Cover: Foto ©ninafisch / pixelio.de

More available books at **www.hansebooks.com**

KINSE SHIRIAKU.

A

HISTORY OF JAPAN

FROM

THE FIRST VISIT OF COMMODORE PERRY

IN

1853

TO

THE CAPTURE OF HAKODATE BY THE MIKADO'S FORCES

IN

1869.

———o———

TRANSLATED FROM THE JAPANESE
BY E. M. SATOW,
Japanese Secretary to H. B. M. Legation.

———o———

YOKOHAMA:
PRINTED AT THE "JAPAN MAIL" OFFICE.
1873.

INTRODUCTION.

It is almost impossible that any person whose attention has been drawn to the extraordinary efforts which the leaders of the Japanese nation are daily making to raise their country to a level in point of moral and material civilization with the Occidental World should remain content with noting merely what is passing around him at the present moment. An analysis of the causes of this desire for progress, which seems to be peculiar to Japan alone among Eastern Nations, would require a far greater knowledge of its past political history and habits of thought than any foreigner yet possesses; but at the same time some light may evidently be obtained from the study of the most recent events. It is a fortunate thing, therefore, that a native writer should have undertaken to compile a work which presents so compact a summary as this does of what has passed since the sudden arrival of the American squadron in 1853 awoke Japan from the almost undisturbed slumber of the last two and a half centuries. To any future foreign historian of the relations between it and the outer world such a work, compiled from the most trustworthy sources, cannot fail to be of the greatest use, and it is chiefly with the object of facilitating such labours that the task of putting it into an English dress has been undertaken.

The author, for what other reason than a dislike to notoriety does not appear, has chosen to conceal his identity in the preface under the fictitious name of 'the rustic annalist of the pepper mountain,' but as he has half revealed it on the title-page, which announces that the work is printed for YAMAGUCHI UJI, there can be no indiscretion in stating that he is an ancient official of the Foreign Department as it was constituted under the administration of the Shôguns, and now an official of the *Mombushô* or Education Department. These two facts are presumptive evidence of impartiality, since to favour the one side too much might be stigmatized as ingratitude for past benefits, while too great leniency to the other would indicate an indifference to present emoluments, somewhat rare.

For the literary merits of the work there is little to be said. It is composed in imitation of the terse style of the Chinese annalists, and is therefore almost incapable of being rendered at once literally and into idiomatic English. Freedom of translation, where the object does not happen to be the illustration of native modes of expression, is always advisable, especially if the idea of the original is thereby more correctly conveyed, and it may be as well to warn students of the language that they must not expect to find here an instrument to aid them in the dissection of Japanese (or rather Chinese) syntax.

Dates on which events occurred are often stated vaguely in the original, the month only being usually given. As the Japanese months seldom coincide with those of the Gregorian calendar (which has only been adopted since the commencement of the current year) it has seemed preferable to translate literally in this instance and to give in brackets the Gregorian dates which correspond to the beginning and end of each month. The precise day, where possible, has been supplied in footnotes from the Genji Yume-monogatari (G. Y. M.), Parliamentary Papers and other sources.

THE TRANSLATOR.

AUTHOR'S PREFACE.

This compilation commences with the arrival of the American squadron in 1853 and ends with the taking of Hakodate in 1869. I have found slight discrepancies in the various accounts of this period which I have seen, and have endeavoured to arrive at the truth by consulting them impartially. I have no doubt, however, that more learned persons than myself will be able to discover mistakes and obscurities in what I have put together in this way, and I shall be grateful for their suggestions.

Public documents and memorials are often of unnecessary length. I have therefore been careful to abridge them as much as possible, so as not to fatigue my reader.

An old axiom says that a historian is worthless unless he possess both native talent, learning and wisdom. As I cannot lay claim to either of these qualifications, there is no doubt that in thus rashly taking up my pen, I expose myself to the accusation of having attempted what is beyond my powers. But there are few complete and authentic histories of modern events. In the one or two works which do exist, the authors have either omitted everything which they thought likely to give offence, or have made their relation so obscure as to render it impossible to understand clearly what the real course of events has been. For this reason I have disregarded my own unfitness for the task, and have recorded summarily what has taken place for the use of those who may hereafter wish to write upon this subject.

SHÔZAN YASHI.

1871.

KINSÉ SHIRIAKU,

OR

SHORT HISTORY OF RECENT TIMES.

VOLUME I.

1. 1853.—In the sixth month (July 5th—August 3rd, 1853. July 7th. G. Y. M.) of the sixth year of Ka-yei, in the reign of the Emperor Kômei Tennô, the American Envoy Perry arrived at Uraga in Sagami with four ships, and handing in a letter, asked for a treaty of amity and commerce. In those days all classes of the nation were so accustomed to a peaceful and enjoyable existence that the suddenness of the event caused great excitement. It was an ancient custom not to allow foreign vessels to enter any port but that of Nagasaki, and this old law was fully explained to the Envoy, who, however, would not listen. The Bakufu [1] eventually received the letter at Shimoda, and ordered the *daimiôs*[2] to guard the most important strategical positions in Musashi. The object of the American mission was then reported to Kiôto, and orders

---

(1) *Bakufu* is the term by which the Shôgunate was usually spoken of by its political opponents. It is derived from *baku*, a curtain (in allusion to the fact of its head being a general, whose camp in Japan was usually surrounded by a curtain) and *fu*, a government office.

(2) Territorial nobles. Although it is somewhat of a barbarism to make the plural of a Japanese work with an English suffix, it is better to do so for the sake of clearness.

were sent by the Imperial Court to the Shintô priests at the shrines of Isé to offer up prayers for the sweeping away of the barbarians.

The American Envoy demanded an answer in the 7th month (August 4th—September 1st), but the Bakufu, explaining how the condition of affairs necessitated its consulting the general opinion of the nation, insisted on a delay. The Envoy was obliged therefore to sail [3] from Uraga, after promising to return the following year. Shortly afterwards the Bakufu communicated the American letter to all the clans, and asked their opinion. Some advocated entering into amicable relations, while others took the opposite view, and maintained that all advances on the part of foreigners ought to be repelled.

In the course of the same month [4] the Shôgun Iyéyoshi died, and was succeeded by Iyésada.

In the 8th month (Sept. 2—Oct. 1) a Russian ship came to Nagasaki and begged leave to enter into friendly relations, in order to discuss the question of the northern boundary between the Japanese territory and their own.

During the same month the ex-Chiunagon of Mito was appointed a commissioner for the superintendence of the maritime defences. In the year 1841 this prince had been placed in confinement at one of his secondary palaces in Yedo for having melted down the bells of all the Buddhist monasteries in his domain to cast cannon with, and for other similar acts, but the Minister Abé Isé no kami now pardoned him by order of the Shôgun, and directed him to make extensive military preparations. The prince had always had two objects at heart, namely an increase of respect for the Mikado and the expulsion of barbarians, [5] and he was celebrated for his energy and courage.

---

(3) July 16. G.Y.M.
(4) August 25. G.Y.M.
(5) In Japanese *son ô, jô i.*

6 Permission to build war vessels was also given in the 9th month (October) to all the *daimiôs*, and the red ball on a white ground, representing the sun, was chosen as their distinguishing flag.

7 The construction of the forts in the sea at Shinagawa was commenced during the same month, and numbers of large cannon were cast. The expenses were met by a contribution levied on Yedo and the villages round and on the rich merchants of Ôzaka.

8 Takashima Shiuhan [6] was released from prison about this time and placed with Egawa Tarozaëmon as musketry instructor. His lessons speedily became fashionable, and the European system of artillery was thus introduced into this country. Shiuhan had learnt the art from a Dutchman at Nagasaki, and its introduction is therefore due to him.

9 1854.—In the 1st month (Jan. 28—Feb. 25) of 1854 [7] the American envoy again arrived with his ships, anchoring this time at Shimoda in Idzu, and demanded the same things as had been urged in the letter presented the previous year. He waited until the 4th month (April 26—May 25), when the Bakufu promised to accord kind treatment to ship-wrecked sailors, permission to obtain wood, water, provisions, coals and other stores needed by ships at sea, with leave also to anchor in the ports of Shimoda in Idzu and Hakodaté in Matsumaë. In the 6th month (June 24—July 23) the envoy left Shimoda, and the same privileges as he had obtained were shortly afterwards granted also to the Russians and the Dutch.

10 Whilst the American envoy was at Shimoda, a Chôshiu man, named Yoshida Shôin, and his pupil Shibuki, suddenly appeared on board of his ship and asked leave to sail with him. The envoy refused and sent them ashore. For this infraction of the laws Yoshida, Shibuki, and

---

(6) Shirôdaiyu and Kihci are other names by which this man is known.
(7) Feb. 18. G.Y.M.

Sakuma Shôzan were cast into prison. Sakuma was a Matsushiro (in, Shinano) man of vast learning, and also acquainted with European literature. He was Shôin's first instructor in the military art. Shôzan had said to the latter: " In these days you should travel in foreign coun-" tries and acquaint yourself accurately with the state of " things there. " At that moment the Bakufu had commissioned the Dutch to construct a man-of-war for it, and Shôzan said ; " Rather than entrust the commission to the " Dutch, send Japanese to Holland to study their most " important arts, and let them purchase a man-of-war by " the same occasion. Besides our countrymen will be-" come expert in navigation as they travel backwards and " forwards, and will learn the condition of all countries. " This would be of immense value to us. " He laid this proposition before the authorities, but it was not favourably entertained. Shôin heard of it, and being mightily taken with the idea, conceived a desire of making a sea-voyage. By chance a Russian vessel put into Nagasaki, and Shôin, pretending that he was merely going there on a visit, but with the secret intention of accompanying her to foreign countries, took leave of Shôzan. Shôzan divined his plan, gave him money for his travelling expenses, and composed a stanza of Chinese poetry in which he wished him a safe and pleasant journey. Shôin then started off direct for Nagasaki, but on his arrival found that the ship had already left. He then returned to Yedo and asked Shôzan's advice about taking passage in the American vessel. Shôzan secretly told him how to set about it, and after the failure of the plan his farewell stanza was discovered in Shôin's trunk, when the latter was arrested, and he was punished as an accomplice. These men were afterwards' sent back to their respective clans and thrown into prison.

In the 7th month (July 24—Aug. 22) * an English

---

(8) Rear-Admiral Sir James Stirling arrived at Nagasaki about the

man-of-war came to Nagasaki and presented a letter, saying: "Hostilities have broken out between our country "and Russia, and we may possibly come to blows with "them in the vicinity of your shores. We may also be "obliged to obtain wood, water and provisions, in which "case we beg you to furnish us with what we "may require." The Bakufu granted permission for this to be done at the two ports of Hakodaté and Nagasaki.

In the 11th month (Dec. 19—Jan, 16, 1855) the [9] sea overflowed its limits at Shimoda in Idzu, and wrecked a Russian vessel which was anchored in the bay. The chronological period was changed this year from Kayei to Ansei.

1855.—In the 3rd month (April 16—May 14) the Court gave orders that the bells of all the Buddhist monasteries throughout the country should be melted down and cast into cannon and muskets, but the Princes of Chionin and Rinnôji opposed the measure, and it was therefore abandoned

In the 4th month (May 15—June 12) the two houses of Sendai and Saraké were ordered to garrison the north, east and west coasts of Yezo.

During the same month Katsu Rintarô was despatched to Nagasaki to learn from the Dutch how to manage steam-vessels.

In the 10th month (Nov. 9—Dec. 7) [10] a great earthquake occurred in the eastern provinces. It was felt most violently at Yedo, where one hundred and four thousand persons lost their lives.

1856.—In the first month of the 3rd year of Ansei (Feb. 5—Mar. 5) the Bakufu commenced to rebuild the Mikado's Palace, which had been destroyed by fire in the previous year as well as the castle at Yedo

---

7th September, and signed a convention with the Japanese plenipotentiaries on the 14th October. Parl. Papers.
(9) December 22. G.Y.M.
(10) November 10. G.Y.M.

and the Shrines [of the Shôguns] at Shiba and Uyéno, which had been destroyed by fire some time before. In olden times, whenever any works of the kind were required, the clans were called upon to contribute towards the expense, but the rule was departed from on the present occasion, in view of the great charges they had been put to during the last year or two in maintaining garrisons at various places. The Bakufu treasury was, however, reduced to a very low ebb.

In the 7th month, (July, 31—August 22) batteries were erected at the two mouths of the Ôzaka river.

During the same month an American named Harris arrived at Shimoda in Idzu, bearing a letter. He stated that he was entrusted by his nation with full powers, and that he was instructed to reside in Japan. He also requested leave to present his credentials to the Shôgun. About the same time an English vessel [11] came again to Nagasaki and commissioned the Dutch to ask permission for them to enter into relations of amity and commerce.

A great storm occurred in the eastern provinces during the 8th month (Aug. 29—Sept. 27), and more than a hundred thousand persons lost their lives at Yedo.

During the same month Hotta Bitchiu no kami was appointed a Minister, with rank above his colleagues. It is said that this was done by the advice of the Minister Abé Isé no kami, who found the burden of state affairs too much to bear, for various portents had occurred during the last two years, and the Bakufu was driven to its wits end by the repeated visits of the foreigners.

1857.—In the first month (Jan. 25—February 22) the chief of the Dutch factory at Nagasaki sent in a letter, saying: " I advise you to be careful, for in intercourse with " foreign countries disputes often arise out of the smallest

---

(11) This is an evident mistake for the visit of Rear-Admiral Stirling in October 1855 to exchange the ratifications of the Convention concluded by him in the previous year.

" matters, let alone questions of right and wrong. To be
" ignorant of your own weakness is certainly not the way
" to preserve your country from danger. It was for this
" reason that China some ten years ago lost part of her
" territory after the opium war, and that the province of
" Kuang-tung is now a desert." The Ministers believed
that this mention by the Dutch of the Canton war was not
a mere exaggeration of the facts, prompted by a desire to
gain their own ends, and they began to fear that if they
excited the wrath of the foreigners beyond a certain point
Japan would bring on herself the same fate as the province
of Kuang-tung. If they were to change the law which had
been in existence since 1639, and to enter into friendly
relations, they would also have to change their method of
treating foreigners, and act in accordance with the practice observed previous to that year. The Bakufu thus
came to the conclusion that it must do its best to preserve peace.

During the same month the ex-Chiunagon of Mito
declared his unwillingness to have any further share in
public affairs. This resolution was attributed to his dissatisfaction with the course pursued towards foreigners
by the Bakufu.

The American Harris, who was residing at Shimoda all
this while, preferred frequent requests for permission to
proceed to Yedo in order to have an interview with the
Shôgun. An ancient custom forbade the entry of foreigners into Yedo, and the Bakufu quoting this, exhausted
every possible art in order to dissuade him from his project. Harris, however, would not listen, and it had no
resource but to give way. When it informed the
princes of Mito, Kishiu and Owari and the princes of the
Extraordinary Council (*Tamari no ma dzumé*), most of
them, especially the ex-Prince of Mito and the Council,
were disgusted, and recorded their opinion in a written
protest.

Harris eventually reached Yedo in the 9th month (Oct. 17—Nov. 15). He had an interview with the Shôgun and presented his credentials, after which he withdrew and returned to his lodgings. Shortly afterwards he had an interview with the Ministers and briefly stated his demands. These were, unrestricted trade between the merchants of both countries in all articles except gold and cereals, without any official interference; the closing of Shimoda and the opening of Kanagawa and Ôzaka; the residence of a minister plenipotentiary at Yedo, to settle all diplomatic questions, and the conclusion of a treaty in detail, to be ratified by the Japanese Government.

1858.—The Bakufu was afraid of exciting hostile comment amongst its own people, and sent Hayashi Daigaku no kami to Kiôto in the 12th month (Jan. 14—Feb. 12, 1858) in order to request the Mikado's sanction, and the failure of this negotiation being reported to Yedo, the Minister Hota Bitchiu no kami was also despatched in the 1st month of the 5th year of Ansei, (Feb. 13—March 13) to explain the critical state of affairs and to ask for sanction. Several of the court nobles (*kugé*), however, sent in a joint memorial to the Mikado, in which they strongly opposed the measure, and the opinion of the court was divided.

In the 2nd month (March 14—April 12) the American Harris, rendered impatient by the long interval which had already elapsed without anything being communicated to him about the treaty, threatened that if his time was to be wasted in this way, he would proceed forthwith to Kiôto and arrange it himself. He was surprised, after being informed that Yedo was the seat of government, to find such dilatoriness on the part of the Bakufu, and he gave it a certain number of days within which it must make up its mind. The Bakufu at once sent messengers post haste to stir up Bitchiu no kami, but from the state of things at Kiôto it was evident that nothing would persuade the Court to give way.

There was a certain retainer of the prince of Hikoné, named Nagano Shiuzen, who happened to be on intimate terms with one Shimada, a retainer of the Kuambaku, Kujô dono, and the Bakufu induced Shimada through Shiuzen to talk the Kuambaku over. The Kuambaku then issued a decree stating that full powers were given to the Bakufu to deal with the foreign question. Sanjô Naidaijin and eighty-eight other Court nobles reproached the Kuambaku for having lightly decided so weighty an affair, and the opinion of the Court undergoing a complete change, the negotiation became a failure. Hotta Bitchiu no kami returned to Yedo in the 3rd month (April 13— May 11).

It was at this time that Ii Kamon no kami was elevated by the Bakufu to the office of Tairô (or Chief Minister).

In the 6th month (July 10—Aug. 7.) an epidemic of cholera spread throughout the land, and about 30,000 persons died in Yedo alone.

The Shôgun Iyésada being childless, Ii Kamon no kami chose Iyémochi, the prince of Kishiu, to be his heir and successor.

During the same month American and Russian men-of-war came to Yokohama and gave information that the English and French squadrons would arrive in a few days with the object of concluding a treaty. Harris took advantage of this to point out what he considered the best course for them to pursue, and to urge the ratification of his own treaty. Ii Kamon no kami began to think that if, in the presence of these constant arrivals of foreigners of different nations, he were to wait for the Kiôto people to make up their minds, some unlucky accident might bring the same disasters upon Japan as China had already experienced. He therefore concluded a treaty at Kanagawa, and affixed his seal to it, after which he reported the transaction to Kiôto. Immediately afterwards the Russians, English and French entered Yedo, and concluded treaties on the model of the American treaty. It was at this time that the agitation for 'expelling the barbarians' was started, and many people began to discuss domestic and foreign affairs.

Some time before this the Shôgun Iyésada had fallen ill, and he eventually died in the 8th month (Sept. 6—Oct. 5).[13] He was succeeded by Iyémochi, who was only twelve years of age. Ii Kamon no kami kept him in his power, and wielded immense authority. He was generally nicknamed 'the swaggering Chief Minister' (*Bakko Genrô*). When a proposal to choose an heir to the late Shôgun was first made the princes of Owari, Echizen and several others advised that Shitotsubashi Giôbukiô, who was a grown man and had both reputation and popularity on his side, should be adopted by the head of the Tokugawa family. Giôbukiô was the eighth[14] son of the ex-prince of Mito, who loved him more than all his other children, but Ii Kamon no kami rejected his candidature, and put in the prince of Kishiu. When the treaties were made, the princes of Owari and Echizen and the ex-prince of Mito, who were much offended at his arbitrary conduct, at once ordered their palanquins and proceeded to the castle. The populace was afraid that an outbreak of a dangerous kind would result from this extraordinary event. The three princes insisted on seeing the Shôgun, in order to argue the matter with him personally, but Ii Kamon no kami refused, and receiving them himself crushed their remonstrances. The three princes retired in a rage, and Ii Kamon no kami forbade them to appear again at the castle. Ii Kamon no kami was devoted to a species of theatrical entertainments called *Nô*, and he

---

(13) August 15th, G.Y.M.
(14) 7th according to the Taihei Bukan, or list of Japanese territorial nobles.

borrowed ten thousand *riô* from the public treasury to defray his expenditure. Every day he had performances and gave himself up to amusement; but when the Court, hearing of the state of affairs at Yedo, summoned him and the three princes to Kiôto, in order to restore peace among them, he reported the circumstances which had led to the disgrace of the princes, and excused himself from appearing on the ground of his multifarious public duties.

During the same month secret instructions were sent from Kiôto to the ex-prince of Mito, which ran thus: " The Bakufu has shown great disregard of public opin-
" ion in concluding treaties without waiting for the opinion
" of the Court, and in disgracing princes so closely allied
" by blood to the Shôgun. The Mikado's rest is disturbed
" by the spectacle of such misgovernment when the fierce
" barbarian is at our very door. Do you therefore assist
" the Bakufu with your advice ; expel the barbarians,
" content the mind of the people, and restore tranquility
" to His Majesty's bosom."

When the princes of Owari and Echizen tried to have Shitotsubashi Giôbukiô adopted as the Shôgun's successor, Ajima Tatéwaki and Aizawa Idaiyu, retainers of Mito, and Ukai Kichizaëmon and his son who were resident at Kiôto, sought counsel in the matter, by order of the Court, from Kobayashi Mimbutaiyu, a retainer of Takadzukasa dono, and Muraöka, one of Takadzukasa dono's women. It happened also that Hashimoto Sanai came to Kiôto upon the same business, and consulted with Kobayashi. They were also assisted by Kusakabé Isôji and Ii-idzumi Kinai at Yedo. Isôji eventually came to Kiôto by Ajima's orders, whereupon they all took counsel together and the negotiations were going on well, when the whole project was ruined by the opposition of Ii Kamon no kami. Isôji was eventually selected to carry the private instructions of the Court to the ex-prince of Mito.

Ii Kamon no kami had some time previously sent his

retainer Nagano Shiuzen to Kiôto as a spy. This man discovered that the secret instructions had been sent, and also got hold of the correspondence of Ajima Tatéwaki and the rest relative to the proposal to make the Gibbukiô heir to the Shôgun. There was also a considerable body of Court nobles' retainers and of Chinese professors who blamed Ii Kamon no kami's conduct in the matter of the treaties, and Shiuzen, having ascertained their names, reported everything to his master. Ii Kamon no kami at once despatched the Minister Manabé Shimôsa no kami to Kiôto, where, after having consulted with Sakai Wakasa no kami, the Shôgun's Resident, he placed Takadzukasa, Konoyé and Sanjô (Court nobles) in confinement, and arresting Kobayashi Mimbutaiyu, Kasuga Sanuki no kami, Moridera Inaba no kami, Takahashi Hiôbu, the woman Muraöka, Ukai Kichizaemon and his son, Hashimoto Sanai, Rai Mikisaburô and Uméda Genjirô, thirty persons in all, sent them to Yedo in the charge of an armed force. Twenty-seven persons, including Ajima Tatéwaki, Kusakabé Isôji, Ii-idzumi Kinai and Fujimori Kôan were arrested at Yedo.

1859.—In the 12th month of the 6th year of Ansei (Jan. 3—Feb. 1, 1859) the office of Shôgun was conferred by the Mikado on Iyémochi.

The ex-prince of Mito had frequently pressed the questions of the necessity of showing due respect to the Mikado and the expulsion of the barbarians on the attention of the Bakufu, which however paid no attention to him, and he finally put his views in writing and forwarded them to Kiôto. In the 8th month (Aug. 27—Sept. 24) the Chief Minister and his colleagues reproached the ex-prince, saying : " When we refused to listen to your " lordship's advice, you laid your views before the Court, " upon which Ajima Tatéwaki abused the Bakufu, alleg- " ing that it misgoverned the country, in order to mislead " the Court nobles. He then privately brought instruct-

"ions to your lordship from the Court, and nearly suc-
"ceeded in bringing about a rupture between the Mikado
"and the Shôgun. Furthermore, when the succession
"question was pending, he obstinately besought the
"Mikado to order the adoption of Shitotsubashi Giôbukiô.
"Although the ostensible actor was Tatéwaki, your lord-
"ship was the real author of these proceedings, and you,
"whose duty is to be the support of the Bakufu, have
"have failed in your obligations." They consequently
placed the ex-prince in perpetual confinement at Mito, and
in order to punish Shitotsubashi for having desired the
office of Shôgun, they forced him into retirement. Shortly afterwards they made the princes of Owari, Echizen,
Tosa and Uwajima resign their *daimiates* to their sons,
and retire into private life at their secondary *yashikis*[15] for
the offence of having shared in the conspiracy. Kobayashi
Mimbutaiyu and twenty others were condemned, some to
exile, and others to imprisonment, while Ajima, the two
Ukai, Hashimoto, Uméda, Rai and others were put to
death.

In the same month Yoshida Shôin of Chôshiu suffered
capital punishment. He had been confined in prison ever
since the Bakufu delivered him to his clan in the autumn
of 1854. During this period his fanatical patriotism
constantly increased, and all his hopes were fixed on forcing the Bakufu to expel the barbarians. Some one having
proposed to make war on the Bakufu, Shôin, who felt
the injustice of such a proceeding, wrote a pamphlet
against the scheme, and was afterwards released from prison. When Ii Kamon no kami assumed the reins of government, and the Bakufu, estranged from the princes who
were blood-relations of the Shôgun, was left without sup-
porters, Shôin declared that it could not be saved. He

---

(15) Every *daimiô* had a *kami yashiki* or chief residence, and one
or more *shimo yashiki* or private residences.

secretly wrote to a court noble named Ôhara Shigétami [16] inviting him down to Chôshiu, in order to get up an agitation in the clan for the expulsion of the barbarians, and the restoration of the Mikado. It happened that Manabé Shimôsa no kami had arrested, by order of the Chief Minister, all the patriots of Kiôto; and Shôin, collecting a number of desperate men, despatched them to the capital to assassinate Shimôsa no kami. The project came to nothing, and the clan, observing that there was something strange in Shôin's proceedings, cast him a second time into prison, fearing to incur the resentment of the Bakufu. Not long afterwards the Bakufu found reason to suspect Shôin, and despatched Nagai Uta [17] to Chôshiu, to bring him to Yedo in a cage. He was then interrogated about his having conveyed an anonymous document into the Palace at Kiôto, and about a secret conspiracy into which he had entered with Uméda, when the latter was on a visit to Chôshiu. Shôin had always been a friend of Uméda's, and knew nothing about the anonymous document. He therefore gave complete explanations on these two points, but confessed his letter to Ôhara and his plot to assassinate the Minister. These matters had been hitherto quite unknown to the Bakufu, which was exceeding astonished when it heard of them, and inflicted capital punishment on Shôin. Every plan conceived by this man since his failure in the attempt to get a passage on board the American squadron had ended in disaster, and his fate excited universal pity. A great number of upright and loyal men lost their lives about the same time, and their fate was compared to that of the learned men of Tunglin under the Ming dynasty.

Kanagawa, Nagasaki and Hakodaté were opened in the

---

(16) This is the elder Ôhara, still alive at the present day (69 years old in 1873), known also as Ôhara Sakingo, Envoy from the Court to the Shôgunate in September, 1863.

(17) Nagai Uta was a Chôshiu man who held moderate views, and wrote a pamphlet to prove that the *daimiôs* owed allegiance to the Shôgun, and not to the Mikado.

summer of this year, and permission was given to Japanese and foreign subjects to trade with each other. In the 10th month (October 25—November 22) that chief Castle at Yedo was destroyed by fire.

1860.—Envoys were despatched to the United States of America for the first time in the first month of the 1st year of Manyen (January 22—February 20, 1860).

When Ii Kamon no kami punished the princes of Owari, Mito and Echizen all classes held their breath and looked on in silent affright. From that moment his power increased daily, but a few *rônins* conspired to assassinate him, and watching for an opportunity, approached his palanquin one day as he was proceeding to the castle, under the pretence of presenting a petition. Snow happened to be falling heavily, and rendered every object indistinct, so that the escort taking the men to be ordinary petitioners, scarcely noticed them. Suddenly the head of the train was attacked, and the commotion which ensued in that quarter drew away the attention of the guards at the side of the palanquin. The petitioner profited by his opportunity to cut down the bearers, and to reach the palanquin, and a number of confederates sprang up instantly, who succeeded in slaying the Chief Minister, and in escaping with his head. The escort engaged the men who had attacked the front of the train, and fought vigorously. Four, including Nagoshi Genji and Kusakabé Naiki, were killed on the spot, while Kusakari and nineteen others were wounded. The affair occurred so suddenly that they were unable to assist their master, and on looking round were horrified to see what had happened. They pursued the *rônins*, but could not overtake them. This affair, known as the Sakurada outrage, occurred on the 3rd day of the month (March 23). [18]

---

(18) In Sir R. Alcock's despatch to Lord Russell of the 2nd April 1860, the attack on the Regent is said to have taken place on the 24th March. As will be seen by reference to this despatch, Sir R. Alcock was still unaware of the result when he wrote, and it is quite possible

The perpetrators of this deed were Ôzéki Washichiro, Sano Takénoské Saitô Kemmotsu, Kuroda Chiuzaburô, Arimura Jizaëmon, and twelve other Mito men. Some were killed, while others escaping to the house of the Minister Wakizaka Nakadzukasa no taiyu, addressed a letter to him in which they enumerated the crimes of Ii Kamon no kami. They accused him firstly of possessing himself of the person of the young Shôgun, and of dismissing and appointing officials as his own selfish objects suggested; secondly, of receiving enormous bribes and granting private favours; thirdly, of having driven away the princes of Owari, Mito, and Echizen, thereby depriving the Shôgun of the support of those who were most nearly allied to him by blood; fourthly, of having deluded His Highness Kujô, by means of Manabé Shimôsa no kami and Sakai, the Shôgun's Resident, besides confining Prince Jôren-In and many Court nobles, and putting numbers of the *Samurai* and common people to death; and fifthly, of being frightened by the empty threats of the foreign barbarians into concluding treaties with them, without the sanction of the Mikado, and under the pretext of political necessity. These five crimes being such as neither the gods nor men could pardon, they as the representatives of divine anger had chastised him. They prayed that death might be at once inflicted upon them, and shortly afterwards underwent capital punishment.

From this time the advocates of the expulsion of the barbarians increased every day, and in the 8th month (Sept. 14—Oct. 12) a motley band of thirty men came to the Satsuma *yashiki* praying the clan to give their support, and to allow themselves to lead the van. The

---

therefore that he may also have been misinformed about the date. Anyone can verify the date given in the text by comparing the European and Japanese almanacs back to the year 1860. The earliest comparative Japanese and European almanac accessible to the translator was that of 1864.

Satsuma clan pacified them, and lodged them for a while within the walls of the *yashiki*.

During the same month a large number of dissatisfied men, who also advocated the expulsion of the barbarians, collected together in Hitachi and Shimôsa. The foreign merchants had been daily arriving in greater numbers at Yokohama, which so increased in wealth and importance as to form a new city of itself. The *rônins* in Hitachi and Shimôsa consequently conceived the idea of attacking it, but the Bakufu issued orders to the neighbouring clans to take every possible precaution. However, the secretary of the American Minister who resided at Yedo, one Heusken[19], was assassinated one evening in Mita as he was returning home from an excursion.

During the 10th month (November 12—December 10) the re-erection of the Shôgun's principal castle at Yedo was commenced.

1861.—During the 1st month of the 1st year of Bunkiu (February 9—March 9) the number of the *rônins* in Hitachi and Shimôsa increased to such an extent that they proceeded into Kôdzuké and Shimotsuké, where, under pretext of requiring war contributions for the expulsion of the barbarians, they extorted money from the peasants and tradespeople. The Bakufu ordered the house of Mito to arrest them.

During the same month some Russians landed in Tsushima under the pretext of repairing their vessel. Sô Tsushima no kami complained of their behaviour to the Bakufu, which despatched some of its officers to bring them to reason and make them leave the island.

In the 5th month (June 7—July 6), some *rônins* attacked[20] the house occupied by the English at Tôzenji in Takanawa. The vassals of the Bakufu and the troops of the Kôriyama clan who acted as guards to the temple

---

(19) Mr. Heusken was murdered on the night of January 14, 1861.
(20) This attack was made on the 29th day of the 5th month or July 5th. Takanawa is the southern suburb of Yedo.

repelled the assailants, and a large number of the *rônins* were killed. The troops of the Bakufu also suffered some loss in killed and wounded, while two of the English were wounded by the *rônins*. The English Minister was angry, and said such ruffians only existed because the Japanese Government could not rule its own country. Remarking that in future it would be useless to appeal to reason with such a people. he retired with the French and Dutch representatives to Yokohama, in order to prepare for an attack with troops. The Bakufu made ten thousand apologies, and the affair, after some difficulties, was peaceably settled. From this time onwards English troops were always stationed at Yokohama, to guard against surprises, and they were commonly called 'the Scarlet Regiment' from the colour of their clothing.

During the same month the Bakufu ordered the House of Mito to arrest the men who had broken into the English temple-residence, but they made their escape into Ôshiu and Déwa.

The ex-prince of Mito died in the 8th month (Sept. 4— Oct. 3). Whilst he was still alive Ii Kamon no kami applied to Kiôto for leave to make him give up the letter of instructions which had been sent to him some years previously by the Court, and his application was granted. Ii Kamon no kami then despatched Andô Tsushima no kami to communicate this to the house of Mito, but the *samurai* refused, believing it to be nothing but an invention of the Bakufu, and hundreds of them were ready to quarrel about the affair. A great commotion ensued in the clan, which the house of Mito had much difficulty in appeasing. The ex-prince, who disliked having to resist the Shôgun's orders, wrote a letter for the information of his retainers, which was so perfectly reasonable that they, withdrew their opposition. Upon this the Imperial letter was given up to the Bakufu.

51 In the 11th month (December 2—30) the Princess
Kazu, younger sister of the Mikado, arrived in Yedo. The
Minister had argued that the marriage of the adopted
daughter of the prince of Satsuma with the previous Shôgun had been evidence of the submissiveness of that great
clan. But he had died early, before any support could be
derived from his consort's relatives. On this occasion they
married the Shôgun to the Mikado's younger sister, in
order to show to the world that the Imperial family and
the house of Tokugawa agreed in their political views.

52 Envoys were despatched this year to [21] England, France,
Russia, Holland, Prussia and Portugal for the first time.

53 1862.—In the 1st month of the 2nd year of Bunkiu
(Jan. 30—February 28) as the Minister Andô Tsushima no kami was going to the castle a number of *rônins*
attacked him in front of the Sakashita gate.[22] His escort
repelled the assailants and Tsushima no kami escaped with
a wound on his shoulder. Several of the *rônins* were
killed, and a document was found on each of them in
which Tsushima no kami was reviled. The substance of
it was: " The Minister Andô, inheriting the ideas of the
" Chief Minister Ii Kamon no kami, has made friend of
" the barbarians. In concert with the Resident Sakai
" Wakasa no kami he has placed in confinement honour-
" able and loyal Court nobles. He has abused the influ-
" ence of the Bakufu in order to bring the Mikado's sister
" to Yedo, and, worst of all, has commanded learned Japan-
" ese scholars to collect precedents for the deposition of
" the Emperor, his intention being to depose the Son of
" Heaven. His crimes are too heinous to be spoken of
" with calmness, and we have therefore sacrificed our
" lives in order to kill this wicked traitor." The Bakufu

(21) The embassy to the Treaty Powers left on the 21st Jan. 1862,
before the Japanese New Year, which accounts for the apparent
misstatement in the text.

(22) This gate stands between the Hommaru or Chief Castle, and
the Nishi no Maru, or western Castle, formerly appropriated to the
heir apparent of the Shôgun, and now converted into a Palace for
the Mikado. The attack took place on the 14th Feb. G.Y.M.

at once deprived Tsushima no kami of his office as Minister, and tried to get into the good graces of the influential court nobles by increasing the official salaries of Kujô, Hirohashi, Bôjô, Asukai, Chikusa, Iwakura and thirteen others.

During this period the *samurai* deserted from their clans in daily increasing number. They allied themselves with the *rônins* in all parts of the country to raise the cry of 'honour the Mikado and expel the barbarian,' thus creating a great ferment throughout the empire. In the 2nd month (March 1—29) the house of Shimadzu published a proclamation to its retainers, expressing approval in the main of the policy of supporting the Mikado, but forbidding them to ally themselves with the *rônins* for the advancement of the objects above-mentioned, or to do anything without the instructions of their superiors.

Not long previously the Prince of Chôshiu, who was in Yedo, had addressed a letter to the Bakufu, saying: "Since the conclusion of the treaties the people of this "empire have done nothing but protest against them. They "declare that you have disregarded the Mikado's wish "that the country should be closed to foreigners, and that "you treat him as if he were not of the slightest import-"ance. I beg most earnestly that the Shôgun will "recognize the supremacy of the Mikado, so that the "harmony existing between the two may be made evident, "and the comments of the people be put a stop to." He added that his retainer Nagai Uta was familiar with the state of opinion at Kiôto, and the Bakufu sent for him to ask his advice. Nagai was altogether in favour of a conciliatory policy, and his advice entirely fitted in with the views of the Ministers. The Bakufu rewarded him handsomely, and proposed to send him to Kiôto with secret instructions, but the very suspicion of his being in the Bakufu's interests greatly diminished his influence with his own clan.

In the 4th month (April 29—May 28) Nagai Uta arrived at Kiôto, furnished with special instructions from the Minister Kuzé Yamato no kami, and addressed a letter to the *Tensô* [23] Nakayama Dainagon, in which he set forth in detail the nature of the circumstances which rendered the Imperial sanction to the treaties so necessary. At this moment the agitation for the expulsion of foreigners arose throughout the length and breadth of the land. A great deal of hostile criticism was directed against Nagai, who was unable to attain his object, and shortly afterwards set out to return to Yedo. The Chôshiu men who were at Kiôto were much offended with his expressed opinions, and lay in wait to assassinate him at Ôtsu on the Tôkaidô. Nagai divined their intentions, and avoided them by starting earlier and taking the route by the Nakasendô. In the following year the Chôshiu clan ordered him to perform disembowelment.

During the same month Shimadzu Idzumi [24] was travelling to Yedo, and had got as far as Himéji in Harima. It happened that a certain Hirano Jirô of Chikuzen, who was lurking in those parts, had caused a good deal of excitement by raising the cry of 'honour the Mikado and expel the barbarians.' He had collected together a body of two hundred sympathetic spirits, and proposed to them that as it was impossible to preserve discipline amongst so motley a society, the best plan would be to place themselves under the leadership of one of the great clans. They were on the look-out for an ally of the kind they wanted, when they heard of the arrival of Shimadzu

---

(23) The *Tensô* were Court nobles appointed to act as mediums of communication between the Court and the Shôgunate. They were generally two in number. The institution of this office is attributed to Yoritomo. *Ten* is 'to communicate' to an inferior; *sô*, 'to report to the Sovereign.'

(24) The father of the Prince of Satsuma, afterwards notorious as Shimadzu Saburô, then known as Shimadzu Ôsumi no kami and now as Shimadzu Jiusammi. He is the younger brother of Satsuma no kami, the previous prince of Satsuma, who having no children of his own, adopted the eldest son of Saburô. Saburô is thus legally only the uncle of the prince of Satsuma—(Prince of Satsuma no longer.)

Idzumi at Himéji. Hirano, who was aware of the intrepid character of this prince, at once proceeded thither with his men and addressed a letter to him. It said: "The Bakufu has lately been treating the Mikado's orders with contempt, and has concluded treaties without his sanction. The Empire is on the point of becoming a hell. We wish therefore to get you to become our leader, in order that we may release the Court nobles who have been confined in consequence of the Bakufu's displeasure, seize the castles of Ôzaka, [25] Hikoné and Nijô, send orders to all the clans, carry the Mikado to Hakoné, punish the crimes of the Shôgun, and immediately afterwards sweep out the barbarians. Pray take our request into your gracious consideration, oh Prince, and grant it." They then asked him to forward their letter to the Imperial Court. Idzumi felt secretly alarmed at their violence, and giving an evasive answer, pacified them as well as he could. Having left them at the town of Fushimi he went on to Kiôto, and sent Hirano's letter to Konoyé (a Court noble). The Court was so frightened at the seditious style of the letter, that it retained Idzumi at Kiôto to keep the *rônins* in order. It happened that the *rônins* at Ôzaka and some Satsuma *samurai* of the same way of thinking heard of this, and were enraged at what they called Idzumi's temporizing policy. Some forty or fifty started for Kiôto at once, intending to put pressure on him, and proceed to action. On receiving this news, Idzumi sent some of his retainers to stop them at Fushimi, and to persuade them to remain quiet. The efforts of the retainers were unavailing, and after a long dispute, they were obliged to use force. Numbers were killed on both sides, and the town became the scene of an indescribable commotion.

---

(25) The castles of Ôzaka and Nijô (at the end of Nijô street in Kiôto) belonged to the Shôgun. That of Hikoné in Omi to the Ii family.

Not long before this the prince of Chôshiu, who was still at Yedo, had addressed a letter to the Bakufu in which he said that the domestic and foreign troubles which threatened the land were entirely destroying the national tranquillity. The Shôgun ought therefore to proceed to Kiôto, and call an assembly of *daimiôs* in order to ascertain the opinion of the nation. All matters concerning the general government of the country ought to be ordered by the Court and the Bakufu in concert, in which case the general opinion would be easily obtained. The Court at once sent for the writer of this letter, and ordered him to undertake the preservation of order among the *rônins* in conjunction with the house of Shimadzu.

In the 5th month of (May 29—June 26) the English addressed a letter [26] to the Bakufu in which they asserted that the Bonin islands did not belong to Japan. However, the Bakufu had already, in the previous year, despatched Midzuno Chikugo no kami thither to ascertain the facts, and they were thus enabled to produce proofs of our title in reply.

On the 22nd day of the 6th month (18th of July)[27] a retainer of Matsudaira Tamba no kami, named Itô Gumpei, one of the guard at Tôzenji, in Takanawa, the lodging of the Englishmen, murdered two of them in the garden, and returning at once to his house committed suicide. The English and their allies demanded satisfaction from the Bakufu, which produced to them the corpse of Gumpei, and made an apology. The charge of maintaining guard was also taken away from Tamba no kami.

Gumpei himself hated foreigners, and, chafing under the idea that his prince should have to protect the objects

---

(26) The despatch here alluded to does not claim the Bonin Islands for Great Britain, but, on the contrary, offers to recognise the right of Japan to those islands so long as the European settlers are not disturbed.

(27) An error for 26th June. The second attack took place on the anniversary, according to the Japanese calendar, of the previous attack, namely, on the 29th day of the 5th month. There is no reason to suppose that this was anything but a coincidence.

of his dislike, had hoped that something would happen to put a stop to it. It happened to be Gumpei's turn to be on guard, and one of the Englishmen having committed an act of discourtesy towards him, he flew into a rage, and took advantage of the darkness to accomplish his purpose.[28]

During the same month the Mikado's envoy, Ôhara Saïmon[29] no kami came down to Yedo and delivered the following message from His Majesty. Firstly, the Shôgun must come up to Kiôto with all the *daimiôs*, great and small, ascertain the opinion of the country, expel the barbarians, and so calm the indignation of the Mikado's divine ancestry. Secondly, five of the greater princes were to be selected, according to the precedent established by Toyotomi Taikô (Taicosama), to be consulted as Chief Ministers upon the conduct of public affairs. Thirdly, Shitotsubashi Giôbukiô was to be appointed guardian to the Shôgun, and the ex-prince of Echizen (Matsudaira Shungaku) to be made Chief Minister of State.[29a] The object of these three measures was the renovation of the institutions created by the founder of the Tokugawa line, and to promote the efficiency of the administration. The Bakufu undertook to carry out these instructions, and determined to go up to Kiôto. Two hundred and thirty years had elapsed since the Shôgun Iyémitsu had last observed this practice, and most people only became aware of the fact that the rule existed for the first time.

In the 7th month (July 27—Aug. 24) the Bakufu dismissed Sakai Wakasa no kami from office, and confined him in his own domains. It also ordered the house of Ii to inflict capital punishment on Nagano Shinzen.

---

(28) The author does not apparently mean that either the unfortunate sentry or corporal of marines who fell victims to the fury of Gumpei was the person who insulted him. It is more than probable that the story of an act of discourtesy having been committed is a fiction.

(29) Also called Ôhara Sakingo.

(29a) According to the G. Y. M. these three alternatives were offered to the Shôgun, and he might accept any of them. It will be seen that the first and third were elected by his advisers.

64 Some time before this the Bakufu, in obedience to the orders of the Court, had released Prince Jôren-In, Takadzukasa, Konoyé, Sanjô, the ex-prince of Owari, Shitotsubashi Giôbukiô, the ex-*daimiôs* of Echizen, Tosa, Uwajima and others from domiciliary confinement. The Shôgun now had frequent interviews, with Owari, Shitotsubashi and Echizen, and passed the time in friendly conversation with them. At the same time Itakura Suwô no kami [afterwards Iga no kami], who was one of the Ministers, made great changes among the officials of the Bakufu. Shitotsubashi was raised from the rank of Giôbukiô to that of Chiunagon, and appointed guardian *(kôken)* to the Shôgun, while the ex-prince of Echizen was made Supreme Director of Affairs *(Seiji-sôsai-shoku)* in accordance with the orders of the Court.

65 In the same month some *rônins* murdered Shimada Sahei and Ugô Gemba, retainers of Kujô dono, at Kiôto, and pilloried their heads on the dry bed of the river at Shijô. The cause of this deed was the fact that these two men had been active associates of Nagano Shiuzen when he was at the capital. The Court therefore punished Kujô, Koga, Chikusa, Iwakura, Tomi-no-kôji and other Court nobles, and appointed Takadzukasa to be Kuambaku. It was generally supposed that these measures were attributable to the misconduct of the above-named persons in the negotiations with Yedo.

66 The prince of Tosa was now in Kiôto, and the Imperial Court, anxious to preserve the tranquillity of the capital, commanded him to act in concert with Satsuma and Chôshiu in the repression of disorder. From this time, whenever the people wished to express the influence and popularity of the princes they always mentioned Sat-chô-to (a compound of the first half of each clan's name).

67 In the intercalary 8th month (Sept. 24—Oct. 22) the Bakufu established an office at Kiôto called *Shingoshoku*

(or Protectorate), and Matsudaira Higo no kami, the prince of Aidzu, was chosen to fill it.

Hitherto it had been a part of the Bakufu's system that the princes should pass each alternate year at Yedo, their wives and children being compelled to reside there continually. The object of this rule was to divide the strength of the clans and to render them easier to keep in order. But in consideration of the great expenditure required from the country the time which they had to pass in Yedo was now lessened, and they were permitted to keep their wives and eldest sons at home in their domains. The style of dress was also reformed, unnecessary ornament being discarded. The prosperity of Yedo, which had in a great measure depended on the residence of the princely families, received a heavy blow from this constitutional change.

During the same month the Bakufu, after enumerating the crimes of the late Ii Kamon no kami, confiscated two-sevenths of the lands belonging to his heir, and punished Andô Tsushima no kami and other adherents of the murdered Minister.

1863.—In the 11th month (Dec. 21—Jan. 19, 1863) Sanjô Chiunagon* and Ané-no-kôji Shôshô came to Yedo as envoys from the Mikado. The message they bore declared that the Bakufu must clear away the old abuses, entirely reform the constitution, and so give peace to the Mikado's mind. Further, that the Shôgun must come up to Kiôto in the following spring, issue his orders to the clans, and proceed without delay to achieve the expulsion of the barbarians.

Shortly before this the Court had ordered the Bakufu to proclaim a general amnesty for political offences. A decree was therefore published throughout the country by which all persons who had been confined for taking

---

* Now (1873) Daijô-Daijin, or Chief Minister of State under the Mikado.

interest in the national affairs since 1858 were released. Pensions were also granted to the widows and orphans of those who had suffered death for their opinions.

During the same month the Bakufu besought the Court to make Toda Wasaburô, a relation of the Toda family of *daimiôs*, commissioner of the Imperial Tombs, and to raise him to the rank of Yamato no kami. Yamato no kami was a man who had remonstrated against these tombs being left in their dilapidated state, and had conducted their restoration.

During the 12th month (January 20—February 17) certain persons unknown set fire to the residence which the Bakufu was erecting for the English at Gotenyama behind Shinagawa.[30] Hanawa Jirô was also assassinated on the top of Kudanzaka. This man had been much detested for having collected precedents for the deposition of the Mikado by the orders of Ii Kamon no kami. The act was generally attributed to men of the Chôshiu clan.

During the same month the House of Shimadzu presented ten thousand *koku* of rice to the Imperial Court.

Some time before, as Nakagawa Shiuri no Daibu was passing through Fushimi on his way to Yedo, Prince Jôren-In and the Court nobles sent a number of *samurai* belonging to various clans to rebuke him for placing Yedo before Kiôto. He thereupon turned back to the capital, and the number of princes who were now assembled there was more than eighty. The city became more crowded than it had ever been within the memory of man.

During this year the Bakufu commissioned Holland to build it a man-of-war, and despatched Enomoto Kamarijô, Akamatsu Daisaburô, Uchida Tsunéjirô and others to that country, to study the art of naval warfare. It also enlisted men belonging to the lower classes to serve as infantry soldiers, and formed its own vassals the Hatamoto into

---

(30) This event happened on the night of February 1. Several men of low social standing who had a share in the work are now high officials of the Mikado's Government.

cavalry and artillery. These troops went by the name of the Sampeitai [31]. Enomoto and those who went with him to Holland made great progress in their studies, and five years later they all returned to Japan with the man-of-war, which was named the "Kaiyô-Maru."

Shitotsubashi Chiunagon arrived at Kiôto in the first month of the 3rd year of Bunkiu (February 18—March 18) whereupon the *samurai* of the different clans and the *rônins* pressed him about the expulsion of the barbarians. He replied that the matter would be settled as soon as the Shôgun should arrive. The *rônins* were disgusted with this temporizing policy, and assassinating Kagawa Hajimé, a retainer of the noble Chikusa, sent the head to the Chiunagon as a blood-offering for the expulsion of the barbarians. They sent the arms to Chikusa himself. Kagawa was a man who in previous times had intrigued with Shimada and Ugô in the interests of the Yedo Government. Todoroki Buhei of Higo and Kusaka Gisuké of Chôshiu also called on the Kuambaku, and urged him to fix a date of the expulsion of the barbarians.

It was about this time that Miwada Kôichirô of the Matsuyama clan and a number of *rônins* cut the heads off some wooden images of Ashikaga Takauji, Yoshinori and Yoshimitsu, [32] which were enshrined at the temple of Tôji-In, and pilloried them in the dry bed of the river at Sanjô. This was intended as a hit at the Tokugawa family, whose acts might be compared to those of the Ashikaga. The prince of Aidzu, offended at this outrage, arrested Miwada and his accomplices. The city was in a commotion, and the prince of Chôshiu interceded for their

---

(31) Lity. three bodies of troops. It would be more convenient in English to call them by the name of 'The Drilled Troops.'

(32) Takauji (b. 1305, d. 1358) was the first Shôgun of the Ashikaga line. His son Yoshinori (b. 1330, d. 1367) did not rise above the rank of Dainagon. He was succeeded by Yoshimitsu, who became Shôgun in 1368 and died in 1408. The insult offered to their effigies occurred on the 9th April. G.Y.M. Ashikaga Takauji at first took the side of Godaigo Tennô against the Hôjô family, but afterwards turned traitor and seized the power for himself.

lives, but the prince of Aidzu and the ex-prince of Echizen were obdurate. From this time onwards the *rônins* entertained great affection for the prince of Chôshiu.

79 In the same month the Court established the Gakujiu-In, which was intended as a place wherein the *samurai* might freely express their opinion on politics. The prince of Kurumé recommended Prince Jôren-In to both the Court and the Bakufu, who permitted him to lay aside his priestly robes. He was henceforth styled Prince Nakagawa, and took part in affairs.

80 In the 3rd month (April 18—May 17) the Shôgun came up to Kiôto and went to Court on the same day, after which he took up his quarters at the castle of Nijô.

81 During the same month the prince of Satsuma[33] addressed a memorial to the Mikado, saying: "For some "time past I have criticised the political situation, and "have offered my humble opinion to Your Majesty. But "the tongue of the slanderer has been busy, and my sug-"gestions have not been carried out. If under these cir-"cumstances I remain at the capital, I am merely justify-"ing the slanders which have been uttered against me, "and I am afraid that some disaster may be the result. "Besides, as the time for the expulsion of the barbarians "is drawing near, I must make my preparations. I beg "therefore that Your Majesty will grant me a few months "leave of absence." Having sent in this letter he departed for Kagoshima on the following day, without waiting for an answer. It was currently reported that he was moved to this course by the remarks which had been made by some of the clans[34] at Kiôto about the assumption by the house of Shimadzu of too large a control over affairs.

(33) When the Prince of Satsuma is spoken of as taking a part in affairs, it must be understood that either Shimadzu Saburô or the leading men of the Satsuma clan acted under his name. Scarcely any of the *daimiôs*, except the ex-princes of Hizen, Tosa, Echizen and Uwajima, were of any personal importance. It is clear in the present instance that it is Shimadzu Saburô who writes.

(34) The word *han*, here translated clan, literally means fence, the duty of a *han* being to defend the throne against its enemies; but clan

During this period the Court deliberated daily upon the expulsion of the barbarians, and finally sent the prince of Mito down to Yedo, to superintend the closing of the ports. All the maritime princes were sent home to their respective provinces to make preparations for war.

The *samurai* of the different clans and the *rônins* had addressed themselves frequently to the ex-prince of Echizen, pressing him about the date for the expulsion of the barbarians. The ex-prince, who knew the difficulty in which this matter was involved, resigned his office of Supreme Director of Affairs, and furtively quitting the capital, returned to his native province.

In the 4th month (May 18—June 15) the Shôgun, Shitotsubashi Chiunagon, the Minister Itakura Iga no kami and other high officials of the Bakufu went to Court. The Mikado thereupon fixed the 25th of June as the date for the expulsion of the foreigners, and ordered the Bakufu to communicate it to all the clans. The Bakufu found itself compelled to obey, but privately resolved to do nothing. The Mikado next proposed to visit Otokoyama,[35] and to deliver to the Shôgun at the shrine of Hachiman the sword emblematic of his authority to expel the barbarians. The Shôgun, however, declined to join the procession, on the ground of sudden illness, but sent Shitotsubashi Chiunagon, who was in attendance on him, to act as his proxy. Shitotsubashi was extremely embarrassed, and suddenly pretexting illness, descended from the shrine. When the *rônins* heard of this they were violently angry, and said: "Bah! this

---

seems the best term by which to denote a fractional part of the nation, which, held together under one chief by the closest ties, looked with hostile eyes on other similar fractions of the nation. As an instance of this feeling it is sufficient to state that a *daimiô's* retainer invariably meant by the term 'my country' not Japan, but the territory ruled over by his lord,

(35) Otokoyama in Yamashiro, also called Iwashimidzu, situated on the left bank of the Yodogawa some fifteen miles from Kiôto, is the site of a celebrated shrine to the memory of Ôjin Tennô, whose worship was there established under the title of Hachiman Daibosatsu. This deified emperor is considered a sort of patron of warriors.

sluggard is not fit for the work." They therefore insisted upon the Mikado's taking the field in person, and asked to be allowed to march in the van. The Court, however, managed to appease their wrath for a while.

During this month the Court appointed the ex-prince of Owari assistant to the Shôgun, while the ex-prince of Hizen was made Superintendent of Civil and Military matters. Shitotsubashi Chiunagon was sent down to Yedo to assist the Prince of Mito in closing the ports.

About this time the Shinchô gumi disturbances occurred at Yedo. There was a Déwa man named Kiyokawa Hachirô in that city, who for some years past had advocated the expulsion of the barbarians. He persuaded one Adzumi Gorô and several others of the same way of thinking to join him in disturbing the peace of Yedo and its vicinity. They had committed several murders, and being hotly chased by the secret police, had fled by way of Echigo into Ôshiu and Déwa, whence they managed to reach Kiôto without detection. The agitation for the expulsion of the barbarians was going on there, and Hachirô tried to egg on the *samurai* of the Satsuma and Chôshiu clans. At this moment the Bakufu was collecting the *rônins* from all parts of the country at Yedo. It gave them pay and formed them into a corps under the name of the Shinchô gumi. Hachirô, profiting by this lucky event, obtained pardon for his previous offences through friends in the Aidzu clan and among the officials, went down to Yedo, and became chief of the corps. The men composing it amounted to five hundred, and there were a large number of lawless ruffians among them. They exacted money from the rich citizens under the name of contributions towards the expulsion of the barbarians, and were preparing to attack Yokohama. Great uneasiness was felt far and wide, and the efforts of the Bakufu to restrain these men were almost ineffectual. At last it issued orders to the clans to arrest them wherever they might be found, and the ring-leaders having been caught, tranquillity was restored. Hachirô is said to have been killed not long after by an Aidzu man named Sasaki.

All this while the Court was daily urging the Yedo Government to close the ports. The prince of Mito, Shitotsubashi Chiunagon and the Minister Ogasawara Iki no kami finally told the foreign representatives resident at Yokohama [36]: "Our people dislike intercourse with for-"eigners, and numbers of them are ready to assassinate "you at any moment. Our Government has done all "that ingenuity could suggest, but the effect of this dis-"like is that the Mikado has ordered us to inform foreign "countries that the ports are to be shut and foreign inter-"course terminated. We beg you to consent." The foreign Representatives replied: "When the treaties "were concluded a compact was made that they were not "to be changed. Why then do you now wish to make a "change? If your country designs such an extraordinary "thing as this, extraordinary calamities will follow. We "are here by order of our respective nations, and have no "authority to decide such an important matter without "referring home. You had better consult our govern-"ments about it, who will decide as they think right." The Bakufu consequently prepared to send ambassadors to foreign nations.

In the 5th month [37] (June 16—July 15) the English came to Shinagawa by sea, having certain requests to

---

(36) This announcement was made by letter on the 24th June, after the indemnities demanded from the Shôgunate for the second attack on the English Legation in 1862, and for the murder of Mr. Richardson had been fully paid. The author has reversed the two transactions.

(37) The negotiation here referred to was commenced at Yokohama in April when a despatch containing the demands of the English Government was sent in to the Shôgunate. The *Havoc* alone proceeded to Yedo on that occasion. The period granted for a definite reply to be given was repeatedly extended, until on the 20th June the English Chargé d'Affaires found himself compelled to place the affair in the Admiral's hands. The *Pearl* and perhaps another vessel were sent up to Yedo, but in the meantime, the Japanese Government consented to all the demands, and hostilities were avoided.

make. When Ôhara went down to Yedo in the previous year as Envoy from the Mikado he was accompanied by Shimadzu Saburô (formerly Idzumi), and on his way back some English people came riding through the head of his train at a place called Namamugi in the province of Musashi. The prince's escort was enraged at this insult and slew the offenders. The Mikado's envoy had just reached the town of Shinagawa, when he heard of the affair. He delayed there for three days in consequence. The English then came with their men-of-war to Yokohama, and addressed a letter to the Bakufu, saying : " Last year you " killed some of our officers. You must arrest the person " who directed this act to be done, and execute him in the " presence of our officers. If you cannot do this, we shall " demand an indemnity of $500,000 from the Bakufu, and " we will also go to Kagoshima and take $30,000 there " also." The letter also fixed a date by which the reply must be given.

As the Shôgun was still at Kiôto the Ministers could do nothing but repeat over and over again that the affair should be adjusted on his return. They also sent a hasty message to the Shôgun, who represented the state of matters at Yedo to the Mikado, and asked for leave to return home. The Court refused to grant it, and the clan of Satsuma, on learning what had occurred, said to the Bakufu : " We hear that the English have demanded the " person of Saburô, a relation of our prince, and that the " government is much embarrassed by their demands. " Saburô says : the English insulted me, and my escort " simply inflicted punishment upon them. But if the " anxiety of the Government can be removed by the Eng- " lish getting hold of me, let it be decided by an appeal " to arms. I certainly will not surrender to them un- " resistingly. This is what Saburô says, and he prays " for the instructions of the Government." The Bakufu, anxious and troubled about domestic and foreign affairs, debated for several months without coming to a conclusion. The English were daily expecting to receive our answer, and the day for the payment of the indemnity was drawing nigh. The Bakufu, fearing that hostilities would break out, issued a proclamation to the townspeople of Yedo, who packed up their property and took refuge in the country round. The commotion was so great, that the Bakufu at last made up its mind, saying: "It looks as if the wrong was on our side in the affair of Namamugi. Let us clear our reputation, and then put an end to foreign intercourse." So it gave the indemnity to the English, who then departed from the Bay of Shinagawa.

For some time past the house of Môri had been constructing batteries at Shimonoséki in Chôshiu, with the object of commencing hostilities against the barbarians. Some Dutch, American and French vessels happening to pass through the straits, our troops fired on every one of them. Several of the foreigners were killed and wounded, while the batteries were destroyed in a visit from a second American vessel. When the order for the expulsion of the barbarians was first issued, the Kokura clan believed that the Bakufu was in reality averse from the measure, and therefore afforded no help to Chôshiu on these occasions. The Court consequently issued a proclamation to the clans observing that it had learnt that certain clans had put their hands in their pockets and looked on quietly when the barbarian ships had been attacked. This had profoundly distressed the Emperor, for, now that a commencement had been made by Chôshiu, it was the duty of all the clans to strive to achieve the work with all possible speed.

During the same month the house of Môri presented ten thousand *riô* in gold to the Imperial Court.

About the same time [38] the Minister Ogasawara Iki no

---

(38) On the 22nd July. G.Y.M.

kami arrived at Ôzaka by sea, and was about to enter the capital, when the Court refused him leave to do so. It proceeded to censure him for his misconduct in paying the indemnity to the English without asking for sanction, deprived him of his rank and titles, and confined him in his *yashiki* at Ôzaka.

In the 6th month (July 16—August 13) the western castle at Yedo was burnt to the ground. It was rebuilt during the following year, and is now known as the castle of Tôkiô.

During the same month the guardianship of the palace gates by the Satsuma clan was discontinued. Some time previously Ané-no-kôji Shôshô had been assassinated one evening in the streets on his way home from the palace. The murderer fled and was not discovered, but common report said that he was a Satsuma man. It was also rumoured that the order above alluded to was given because the Court secretly disliked the Satsuma clan for the murder of the Shôshô.

In the 7th month (August 14—Sept. 12)[39] the English came with ten men-of-war to Kagoshima in Satsuma, saying: "Although the affair of Namamugi is settled so "far as regards the Japanese Government, we must have "twenty thousand dollars from your clan for the support "of the widow and orphans of the murdered official. We "also ask why you killed an Englishman." The Satsuma clan was about to reply when the English seized the men-of-war belonging to the clan without the slightest provocation. A great storm was raging at the time, and the troops seized the opportunity to repel the enemy. Several artillery engagements ensued in which the English ships were severely knocked about and had to retire. They burnt the town of Kagoshima before leaving. After a short interval had elapsed the English began to prepare

---

(39) The squadron arrived before Kagoshima on the 12th August and left on the 17th. £25,000 was the indemnity demanded from Satsuma.

for a second attack, upon which the house of Shimadzu sent men to Yokohama to pay over $20,000, which they borrowed from the Bakufu, and the affair was peaceably arranged. When our troops fired on the English ships, the crews were in such a hurry to escape that one vessel had no time to get in its anchor, so the cable was cut and the anchor left behind. Our troops seized it, and handed it over at the earnest request of the English. When the English get hold of an enemy's anchor they proclaim the fact everywhere, to show how they have gained the victory. The enemy bitterly feels the disgrace, and when peace is made, often pays large sums of money to recover the article. But as the English got back their anchor without the expenditure of a single 'cash they were moved to admiration for Japanese magnanimity.

Shortly before this Shitotsubashi had addressed a letter to the Mikado in which he said: "I have been the un-"worthy recipient of Your Majesty's boundless favours, "and have received the office of Guardian to the Shôgun. "But I have been completely unsuccessful, and feel most "uneasy in my mind. Your Majesty has also specially "instructed me to arrange for the closing of the ports, "but though I have striven day and night to requite one "ten-thousandth part of the benefits I have received from "Your Majesty, I have been unable to carry out that "measure also. My guilt in accepting such a grave re-"sponsibility, without duly appreciating the action of "events and estimating my own capacity, is too great to "escape unpunished. I pray Your Majesty, therefore, by "an exercise of that great goodness which is Your "Majesty's chief attribute, to release me from the office of "Guardian to the Shôgun." The Court had always placed great confidence in the Chiunagon, and therefore refused to grant his request.

The prince of Aidzu was rewarded by the Court with a sum of money in gold and a war surcoat for his services in protecting the capital, and the Shôgun was allowed to return to Yedo.

98 When the Court decided upon expelling the barbarians some of the princes declined to obey. The *rônins*, also, had been active in seditious intrigue, and the Court began to feel secretly alarmed. From this time onward it began to believe in the Bakufu.

99 During this month the Bakufu despatched envoys to Chôshiu, to reprimand the clan for having fired on foreign vessels without orders. The Chôshiu people insisted that they had only obeyed the instructions of the Court and the Bakufu, justified their proceedings, and refused to acknowlege themselves in the wrong. Eventually they forcibly detained one of the envoys named Nakané, and as he did not return, it was believed that he had been assassinated by them. From this moment a breach was formed between the Bakufu and Chôshiu. Some of the court nobles supported the former; others detested Chôshiu for its high reputation. Another party occupied a neutral position, but the Court cherished a secret dislike to the clan.

100 A short time previously the Chôshiu clan had besought the Mikado to make a progress to Yamato in order to show to the Empire his intention of taking the field in person against the barbarians. The proposal was accepted, and public notice was given that he would proceed to open the campaign in person. Some, however, remonstrated, saying that Chôshiu merely wished to get possession of the Mikado's person in order to be able to dictate to the Empire. This accusation caused the Court and the Bakufu to regard Chôshiu with suspicion, and they became desirous of excluding him from a share in the councils of the Mikado. On the night of the 18th day of the 18th month (30th September) Prince Nakagawa, the Prince of Aidzu, with certain court nobles and men of the military class assembled together, and proposed to dismiss Sanjô

and six other Court nobles and the Chôshiu clan. Fearing an outbreak they hastily gave orders to all the clans in the capital to guard the palace gates most vigilantly. The town was thrown into a state of violent commotion and the public anxiety became great. Môri Sanuki no kami, prince of a subordinate Chôshiu clan, and Kikkawa Kemmotsu knew nothing of what was intended, until they saw the excitement of the citizens, and imagining that a revolution must have broken out at the palace, hastened thither with all speed. Admission was refused to them, and their men were removed from the guardianship of the Sakai machi gate, which was placed in charge of the house of Shimadzu. The two clans of Satsuma and Chôshiu, though devoted to the cause of the Mikado, had all along been on bad terms, and this occurrence showed that they were not likely to act any further in conjunction.

Prince Nakagawa was at the side of the throne, and assembling Konoyé, Tokudaiji and other nobles, said: "Sanjô Chiunagon and his friends, adopting the violent "views of the Chôshiu men, have falsified the wishes of "the Mikado, and have given out that His Majesty in-"tended to go to Yamato in order to take the field in per-"son against the barbarians. His Majesty is deeply "offended with them. The Chiunagon and his friends "have plotted high treason with the Chôshiu men." Orders were then issued that the Imperial progress should not take place, and a resolution was taken to punish Sanjô and the other six Court nobles.

The Chôshiu *samurai*, discovering on the 18th (Sept. 30) the change which had occurred in the policy of the Court, made their preparations and departed for their native province, and the seven nobles fled with them. The Court thereupon deprived the latter of their titles and rank, punished eighteen other official court nobles who had been acting in concert with Chôshiu all along.

and prohibited the Môri family from entering the capital. Troops were levied in the surrounding provinces, and measure were taken for the defence of the city. A proclamation was also issued, which declared that many of the decrees lately promulgated were from the mixture of truth and falsehood in them calculated to mislead the people. But those which appeared after the 18th (30th Sept.) were to be considered as genuine expressions of the Mikado's will.

About the same time Matsumoto Kenzaburô, Fujimoto Tesséki and Adzumi Gorô took up arms in Yamato. These men had previously been wandering about from place to place in Yamato and Kawachi, and advocating the expulsion of the barbarians. They were joined by a court noble named Nakayama Tadamitsu, who had absconded from the capital some time before because the dilatory policy of the Bakufu disagreed with his own anti-barbarian views. Nakayama was elected commander-in-chief by this band of men, who now numbered a thousand strong, and styled themselves the "Tenchiu-gumi." [40] Pretending to act by orders of the court they sent detachments, to Sayama, Tannami, Shiraki and other places in Kawachi, to talk over the *daimiôs* and borrow muskets, cannon, saddlery, etcetera, from them. Having crossed by Chihaya they arrived during this month at Gojô in Yamato, attacked the residence of Suzuki Gennai, the Collector, murdered him and five subordinate officials, seized all the rice, weapons and ammunition they could find, and established their head-quarters there. They were prompted to these acts by Gennai's refusal to comply with their orders. Proceeding next to inform the people of the locality that the Mikado was about to make a progress into the province, they declared the country round Gojô to be Imperial territory, and remitted one half of the land-tax, in order to become popular with the inhabitants.

---

(40) Lity. the Heaven's chastisement band.

Before they had been long at Gojô they received information that the policy of the court had undergone a change. Matsumoto and his companions debated together, saying: "Seeing the turn which affairs have taken, the "Bakufu will assuredly punish us. Rather than sit down "to await its attack, let us make one desperate effort." On the morning of the 9th October therefore a detachment of five hundred men attacked the town of Takatori, also situated in the province of Yamato. The troops of Uyémura Suruga no kami, prince of the domain, defended it. The attack was so fierce that the *rônins* almost succeeded in forcing an entrance, but the garrison fought so valiantly that they eventually repulsed the Tenchiu-gumi, and made fifty prisoners. The Tenchiu-gumi retreated to the hills near Amanogawa-tsuji and placed pickets all round them.

The Bakufu had already ordered the clans of Kishiu, Hikoné, Tôdô and Kôriyamaa to march against the rebels, and Midzuno Tamon, the Kishiu commander, led his troops to the attack on the 18th October. The assault was received with a well directed fire of musketry. Tamon received a bullet-wound, and lost a good many of his men. On the 20th Tôdô Shinshichi, the Tôdô commander, advanced against Amanogawa-tsuji with five hundred men. The Shinchiu-gumi had planted an embuscade, and pretended to take to flight, and as Tôdô's troops, who fancied the victory already won, advanced and fell into the trap, they arose on all sides, and routed the advanced body; but the Hikoné troops coming up to the rescue, the united forces finally succeeding in repulsing the *rônins*, whom they pursued as far as Totsugawa. Hereupon the victors withdrew from the field of battle, as the sun was setting. During the evening the Tenchiu-gumi surprised the Hikoné quarters, and retreated again after inflicting a loss of thirty killed.

On the 25th the Tôdô troops fell upon the rear of the

Tenchiu-gumi, and succeeded at last in capturing the stockade of Amanogawa-tsuji. The *rônins* dispersed, but detachments of the Kishiu, Hikoné and Kôriyama troops pursued them far and wide, inflicting a sanguinary defeat on them. Matsumoto Kenzaburô, Fujimoto Tesséki and others were killed. Nakayama Tadamitsu fled to Ôzaka, while Adzumi Gorô and fifty more were made prisoners. The common name for this outbreak was 'the disturbances of Gojô.'

Hirano Jirô, who was at Kiôto before this event, had obtained leave to try and pacify the Tenchiu-gumi. He proceeded accordingly to Gojô, and had been there some time when he heard of the change which had occurred at Kiôto on the 30th September, and he at once returned thither, to pray the Mikado to re-admit the seven court nobles and the house of Môri to the capital. The Court paid no attention to his petition, and Jirô, perceiving that everything was arranged as Prince Nakagawa and the prince of Aidzu pleased, went off to Chôshiu. Here he got hold of one of the seven nobles named Sawa, and with the object of renewing the agitation in favour of the Mikado's opening the campaign in person, went to Ikuno in Tajima in the 10th month (November 11—December 10) with no more than one hundred soldiers under his command. Having proclaimed the crimes of the prince of Aidzu, he was preparing to enter Kiôto to present a petition to the Mikado. He began by attacking the residence of the local Collector in order to provide himself with the funds necessary for the accomplishment of his object, and seized all the money and rice to be found there. But the peasants arose on all sides and attacked him, while the Bakufu sent orders to the neighbouring clans to take the field. His followers occupied Miôkenyama, and fought valiantly for three days until they could hold out no longer. Some were killed, while others fled back into Chôshiu with Sawa. It will be remembered that in 1862

Hirano Jirô assembled together a number of hot-headed spirits, and tried to force Shimadzu Saburô to commence the great work, but that he was placed in confinement in his native province because of the seditious nature of the project. The Court had sent for him in the previous part of the year, and had appointed him chief of the Gakujiu-In. Having absconded from Kiôto before, he was now captured by the troops of Sengoku.

During the course of this month Shimadzu Saburô arrived again at Kiôto, and had an audience of the Mikado on the same day, to urge the necessity of a second visit from the Shôgun and Shitotsubashi Chiunagon. Probably he wanted to take counsel with them.

In the 11th month (December 12—Jan. 8) the Mikado appointed Prince Nakagawa President of the Censorate (*Danjô-no-In*). Henceforth he went by the name of the In no Miya. The Bakufu also increased his allowance, and gave him a thousand bags of rice annually in addition.

During the same month the Chief Castle at Yedo was burnt a second time, and it has never been rebuilt since.

About this time the Court dismissed Takadzukasa from the office of Kuambaku, and appointed Nijô in his stead. Shortly before this, when the Bakufu was about to shut the ports, it represented to the Mikado that it was afraid of the clans proceeding to commit acts of violence, and the Court now issued an order to the princes, directing them to wait for instructions from the Bakufu. The latter then despatched Ikéda Chikugo no kami on a mission to foreign countries to discuss the closing of the ports. The advocates of the expulsion of the barbarians were dissatisfied on hearing of this, feeling that the Court was becoming retrograde in its policy, and fled in a body to Chôshiu.

END OF VOL. I.

VOLUME II.

1864.—During the twelfth month (Jan. 9—Feb. 7)[41] a Satsuma merchant vessel, which had anchored off Tanoura in Buzen on her way from Hiôgo to Nagasaki, was fired on from the forts on the opposite shore of the strait, the Chôshiu people mistaking her for a foreign vessel on account of her build. Thirty Satsuma men were killed, and the resentment of the clan was great.

Shitotsubashi Chiunagon went up to Kiôto during the course of the same month.

In the first month of the first year of Genji (Feb. 8—March 7) the Shôgun proceeded a second time to Kiôto, where he was joined immediately afterwards by Echizen Chiujô. On the 28th February the Shôgun went to Court accompanied by Shitotsubashi Chiunagon and Aidzu Chiujô, and the In no Miya addressed him on behalf of the Emperor as follows: "We are not in favour of a hasty "and ill-considered attempt to expel the barbarians, but "Fujiwara no Sanéyoshi[42] and others, wilfully blind to "the actual condition of affairs in the Empire, have mis-"represented Our Will, have proclaimed the expulsion of "the barbarians without being properly authorized to do so, "and have stirred up war against the Bakufu. The turbu-"lent retainers of the Saishô of Nagato have made a fool "of their lord, they have fired on barbarian vessels with-

(41) Feb. 1. G.Y.M.
(42) The Court Noble Sanjô Chiunagon, now (1873) Prime Minister.

"out provocation; they have murdered the envoy sent to
"their prince by the Bakufu, and finally seduced Sanéyo-
"shi and his companions to follow them down to their
"native province. These fellows must be punished.
"Nevertheless the true cause of these evil deeds is our
"own want of virtue. Henceforward do you assist us in
"carrying out our wishes, by restoring domestic harmony
"to the country and cutting off foreign intercourse." By
speaking thus, after having previously proclaimed the expulsion of the barbarians, the Court brought upon itself the reproach of inconsistency.

95. In the 2nd month (Mar. 8—Apr. 5) Satsuma proposed to despatch an envoy to Chôshiu to demand satisfaction for the merchant-vessel having been fired upon in the end of the previous year, but the Bakufu persuaded him not to do so, promising to obtain redress for him.

96. During the same month Shimadzu Saburô, father of the prince of Satsuma, was raised to the rank of Sakonyé no Shôshô, and associated in the direction of affairs at Court. The rank of *Sangi* (Counsellor-of-state) was offered to Aidzu Chiujô, but he refused it.

97. In the 4th month (May 6—June 3) the office of Guardian to the Shôgun was taken from Shitotsubashi Chiunagon, who was appointed Protector of the Imperial Palace and Commander-in-chief of the Maritime Defences in the Bay of Ôzaka.

98. In the same month the Bakufu presented a new law containing five articles to the Imperial Court; firstly, the Bakufu would provide two thousand bags of rice towards the expenses of the Shrines at Watarai in Isé: that the Shôgun and *daimiôs* on succeeding their repective predecessors should present themselves at Court and acknowledge the bounty of the Emperor; thirdly, that all the western *daimiôs* should pay court at Kiôto, on their way to Yedo; fourthly, that all the clans should make annual presents of their produce to the Emperor, and fifthly, that

playing on musical instruments should be stopped for a certain number of days after the death of a prince of the blood. All these things were done to honour the Court, which consequently gave its consent.

In the fifth month (June 4—July 3) the Imperial Court formally placed the direction of affairs in the hands of the Bakufu, which was also ordered to punish Chôshiu and the seven runaway nobles. On the 23rd of June Shimadzu Saburô returned to Kagoshima, whilst the Shôgun made his way back to Yedo.

During the same month certain retainers of the Prince of Mito, named Fujita Koshirô, and Tamaru Inanoyemon with others, took up arms in Hitachi and Shimotsuké, with the avowed object of expelling the barbarians.

To go back some years;—In the period called *Tempô* (1830—43) the ex-Chiunagon of Mito had selected Fujita Tôko, a certain Toda, a certain Imai and others from among his retainers, and with their aid had inaugurated great reforms in the administration of the clan. At that time Yûki Toraji, a *Karô* [43] of the clan, a man of crafty and intriguing nature, and who had obtained great influence with the ex-Chiunagon, had a greater voice in the Government of the clan than any other, and was extremely averse from changes in the system of administration. He consequently was highly annoyed at the recent elevation to power of Fujita and his associates, and exerted himself to obstruct their reforms. Having been dismissed for this by the ex-Chiunagon, he secretly informed the Bakufu that military preparations were being made in the clan. Some time previously the ex-Chiunagon and Fujita had proposed to abolish Buddhism, thereby incurring the hostility of the bonzes, who circulated a report that the ex-Chiunagon was forming ambitious schemes. The Bakufu therefore placed the ex-Chiunagon and Fujita in domici-

---

(43) The principal retainers of *daimiô* were called *karô*, or 'old men of the family.' It was a hereditary office.

liary confinement, and Yûki regained his share in the administration of the clan. From this moment Yûki and Fujita headed two opposite parties, that of the former being called the Wicked Party (*Kantô*), while that of the latter was known as the Righteous Party (*Seigitô*). Subsequently the ex-Chiunagon was pardoned, and associated in the councils of the Shôgunate, upon which he punished Yûki a second time, and restored Fujita to his former position. From this time onwards the Righteous and Wicked Parties constantly quarrelled with each other, hardly a day passing away quietly. Fujita and the ex-Chiunagon having shortly afterwards died in quick succession, the power fell into the hands of Ichikawa Sanzayemon and Asaina Yatarô of the Wicked Party. Fujita Tôko's son Koshirô, Tamaru Inanoyemon, Tanaka Genzô and their friends were extremely angry, and under the pretence of carrying out the views of the ex-Chiunagon, loudly professed the combined policy of 'honouring the sovereign and sweeping out the barbarians,' hoping thereby to get the upper hand of the Wicked Party.

To resume the thread of our narrative; Fujita and his associates took the field with three hundred men, carrying with them the monumental tablet of the ex-Chiunagon, and coming to Ôhirayama by way of Utsunomiya, ordered the towns-people of Tochigi to supply them with the funds which they required in order to carry out their design of expelling the barbarians. The towns-people, unwilling to submit quietly to this demand, reported the outbreak to the Bakufu, which gave orders, to the clans in the vicinity to chastise the rioters. The troops of Arima Hiôgo no kami " hastened to the scene of disorder, and fought with them in seven encounters, in which neither side was victorious. The rioters then set fire to the town of Tochigi, and the inhabitants took to flight. In the 6th month (July 4—August 1) they arrived at Tsukuba yama in the

---

(44) Fukiagé in Shimotsuké; 10,000 *koku*.

province of Hitachi, where they constructed a stockade to protect themselves from attack. Ichikawa and others of the Wicked Party, having asked leave of the Prince to attack the rioters, the Bakufu, to whom he referred their request, concerted measures with them, and joining forces they attacked the rebels at Tsukuba yama. The latter were however so ferocious in their resistance that they bore all before them, and the news brought from Yedo day after day to Shitotsubashi Chiunagon, the Military Governor of Kiôto (prince of Aidzu) and the Ministers of state was most disheartening.

3 The Chôshiu people had several times addressed letters to the Imperial Court, in which they endeavoured to explain their conduct since the middle of the previous year, but the Court had refused to receive them. During the same month (July 4—August 1) Fukubara Echigo, a Chôshiu *Karô*, arrived at Ôzaka by sea, and proceeded to Fushimi, whence he addressed a letter to the Court, which ran somewhat as follows: " Since the Prince and " his Son obeyed His Majesty's desire that the barbarians " should be expelled, they have passed their days and " nights in ceaseless anxiety lest they should fail in car- " rying out his sacred will, and the whole clan is unable " to understand why the Court should attribute guilt to " Sanjô and his companions. It therefore humbly prays " that the seven nobles may be restored to their functions, " and that the Saishô and his Son may be permitted to " re-enter the capital." Having sent in this letter he endeavoured to get up a fresh agitation at Court for the expulsion of the barbarians. The Bakufu ordered him to send away the part of his men, and to wait where he was for further orders. A short time afterwards the *Karôs* Kunishi and Masuda also arrived at the head of several hundred men, Kunishi encamping at the Temple of Tenriuji at Saga in the vicinity of Kiôto, and Masuda taking up his quarters at Tennôji in Yamazaki.

104   Kiôto at this moment was full of the troops of various clans, who guarded the Nine Gates, leading to the Imperial Palace. The In no Miya, Shitotsubashi Chiunagon, Aidzu Shôshô and the rest declared that the appearance of the Chôshiu men with troops was nothing but an attempt to coerce the Court, and in their rage asked the Emperor's permission to attack them. Shitotsubashi, Satsuma, Echizen, Aidzu, Kuwana, Ôgaki, Hikoné and others ordered their troops to be in readiness to take the field, and the inhabitants of Kiôto, seeing that a conflict was imminent, packed up their property and sought safety in flight.

105   The Chôshiu forces at Saga, Yamazaki and Fushimi, hearing what was in store for them, resolved to anticipate their enemies. Having laid their plans for a sudden attack, which was to result in removing the Aidzu clan and the other evil advisers of the Emperor from his side, they marched straight on Kiôto on the 20th of August before the day broke. The Saga troops entered first, the Commander-in-chief Kunishi advancing against the Nakadachiuri Gate, and the Colonel Kijima against the Shimodachiuri and Hamaguri Gates. Shitotsubashi's troops engaged the front files of Kunishi's force, but were put to flight, and the latter reached the Hamaguri Gate, through which Kijima's men had already forced their way into the Palace enclosure. Here they vigorously attacked the Aidzu troops, and had nearly defeated them, when the Satsuma forces arrived on the spot, and took them in flank. The Chôshiu men were shaken, and forced out of the Hamaguri Gate, on which Kijima rallied his men and renewed the fight with such desperation that he retrieved this temporary check. Kunishi's men then endeavoured to combine their efforts with those of Kijima's men, but one Niré, a Satsuma Colonel, falling on his rear with two hundred men, called his attention in another direction, and the Shitotsubashi troops, plucking up courage, returned to the fight. The Chôshiu men were thus caught between two fires, and were at last put to flight.

106 The Chôshiu force at Yamazaki, consisting of five hundred men under the command of Kuzaka Gisuké, Iriyé Kuichi and Maki Idzumi no kami, arrived later than the Saga division, and seized the palace of Takadzukasa, where the troops of Echizen, Hikoné and Kuwana attacked them without success. They then advanced, and were just about to enter the Imperial Garden when the Satsuma and Aidzu troops arrived in hot haste, and assisted the three former clans in defending it. The bullets of the contending forces fell as thick as hail, and the fight lasted during four hours, at the end of which the Takadzukasa palace was burnt and the Chôshiu forces were defeated with great slaughter. Kuzaka and his colleagues were killed, while the survivors took to flight.

107 In the defeat of the Saga division, Kijima, one of its best officers, received a bullet wound. He fell from his horse and expired. Kunishi barely escaped with his life.

108 The Fushimi division had started thence in the middle of the night to attack the capital. The Hikoné troops attempted to bar their passage, but were attacked and forced to retreat. Profiting by this success the Chôshiu men advanced in a body with drums beating, but falling into an ambush of matchlock men which the Ôgaki colonel Obara Nihei had planted by the side of the road, were put to flight with many killed and wounded. Their commander Fukubara Echigo barely escaped with his life.

109 In this way the three divisions were prevented from effecting a junction in the city, the greater part of which was consumed by the conflagration which accompanied the conflict. Many of the residences of the *kugés* and *daimiôs* were burnt, and an unusual number of men were killed and wounded on both sides, so that the roads were strewn with dead bodies. When the Yamazaki division of the Chôshiu force started, the commander Masuda was left behind with a hundred men to act as a reserve, and upon the main body being defeated, Maki Idzumi no

kami escaped back to inform Masuda and his men of the result. He made Masuda take to flight, preferring himself to die there. Later on when the Satsuma troops who were sent in pursuit arrived at Saga they did not find a single Chôshiu soldier, and returned to Kiôto after having burnt the quarters which had been occupied by the Chôshiu troops.

110   On the following day the Aidzu and Kuwana troops attacked Yamazaki. Maki Idzumi no kami and the fifty men with him fought desperately for a while, and then perished by their own hands, after having set fire to their quarters. On the 29th of August the Bakufu expressed its thanks to all the clans which had contributed to the victory, and obtained an increase of rank from the Mikado for the various *daimiôs* who had headed them. Adzumi Gorô, Hirano Jirô and others who had been imprisoned for their share in the outbreaks at Gojô in Yamato and Ikuno in Tamba were decapitated, and their heads were exposed in public.

111   During the same month Ikeda Chikugo no kami and the other members of his Embassy returned from Europe. They had been sent in the previous year on a mission to the various countries bearing the order for the closing of the ports, and arriving first in France proceeded to explain the object with which they were sent. The French rejected their proposals and refused an answer. The eyes of Ikeda and his companions were opened by the high state of material and moral prosperity which surrounded them, and they returned, without proceeding any further on their mission, to report the failure of their attempts at persuasion. The Bakufu reprimanded them for having disgraced their functions, and reducing their incomes, forced them to retire into private life.

112   In the 8th month (September), the Bakufu begged the Imperial Court to deprive the Môri family and its branches of their titles, in consequence of the attack made

by the Chôshiu[45] clan upon the Palace, and issued an order to all the other clans to march to the chastisement of the two provinces of Nagato and Suwô. Owari Dainagon was appointed commander-in-chief, while to the troops of Satsuma and twenty other clans were allotted the points against which they were to move. With the object also of making preparations for the Shôgun to take the field in person, the *hatamoto* (vassals of the Shôgunate, not being *daimiô*) were brigaded, and orders were given to lay in stores of provisions along the line of march.

113 Before this the foreign representatives at Yokohama had been holding daily councils of war with the object of despatching their ships against Chôshiu, and on hearing of the orders issued by the Bakufu, determined to be first in the field. They therefore attacked Akamagaséki (or Shimonoséki) in Chôshiu with eighteen vessels of war on the 5th September, and fired against the shore. The shore replied by firing at the ships. Cannon balls flew about everywhere, and the smoke of the guns, covered the surface of the sea, until sunset caused both parties to withdraw.

114 On the following day the ships returned and opened a heavy fire on the batteries, from which the gunners were compelled to withdraw. The foreigners then landed, and occupying the hills on the 7th harassed our troops. Our men fought with enthusiastic bravery in several encounters, with varied success, but their ammunition being exhausted they had no resource left but to propose a cessation of hostilities. The foreigners found fault with their conduct in the previous year, but the Chôshiu army produced certified copies of the orders which they had received from the Imperial Court and from the Shôgun, upon which peace was restored. The foreigners then

---

(45) Chôshiu is the Chinese name for Nagato, by which both that province and the *daimiô* of Hagi in Nagato are usually designated.

came to Yokohama and made demands on the Bakufu, saying: "We expect to get an indemnity of three million "dollars for this business. We will be guided by your "decision whether we shall go back to Chôshiu and take "it, or whether the Japanese Government will undertake "to receive it and give it to us." The Bakufu replied:—"Our Government will take it from Chôshiu and "give it to the nationalities interested." This settlement having been arrived at, the foreigners pressed every day for payment of the indemnity, and the Bakufu was at its wit's end.

At the same time the troops of the Bakufu and of Ichikawa were daily attacking Tsukuba yama. Fujita and his friends fought with fierce desperation, but from the want of discipline among the men, and the contradictory orders given, many chances were thrown away, while the forces of the Bakufu attacked them vigorously and rendered their position less hopeful every day.

Ichikawa and his party gradually acquired greater power, owing to the support given to them by the Bakufu. They hated the Righteous Party, whose members they either placed in confinement or dismissed from office. The Righteous Party, unable to endure this persecution, determined to proceed to Yedo and complain to their prince. With this object three hundred men quitted their homes and reached Koganei in Shimôsa, where entry into Yedo was refused to them by the Bakufu, which ordered their prince to pacify them. At this moment Takéda Iga happened to be in Yedo, and begged leave to undertake the service of pacifying the two parties, and the Prince, knowing that Takéda had been regarded with much favour by the ex-Chiunagon, on account of his belonging to the Righteous Party, requested permission from the Bakufu to send him. The Bakufu therefore despatched Matsudaira Ôi no kami, the head of a cadet family of Mito, and attached Takéda Iga to him. Ôi no kami, Takéda and his companions arrived in Mito at the head of the Koganei men on the 10th September, and were about to enter the Castle, where Ichikawa and his friends refused to admit them, on the ground that they belonged to the other Party, and having posted their troops all about the neighbourhood, waited to see how Takéda would act. Takéda tried to repulse them in order to proceed on his way, whereupon the matchlockmen of the Wicked Party opened fire upon him in concert, throwing his men into confusion; and following up their advantage, forced him to retreat. He was compelled therefore to carry off Ôi no kami and flee to Iso-nohama, where after holding a council of war, he attacked the Wicked Party at Iwafuné yama on the 12th. Kawakami, the commander of the Wicked Party, was killed, together with ten of his men, and the remainder of the force retreated from Iwafuné yama to the port of Naka.

Takéda and his friends crossed the river on the 16th and advanced against Naka, which they took and occupied after exchanging a few shots with the enemy. Ichikawa revenged himself by denouncing Takéda and his friends as criminals, and complained to the Bakufu, after which he arrested and threw into prison the wives and children of Takéda's followers who were in the town. He then attacked Takéda himself, but the troops of the latter fought with great courage, and the losses were equal on either side.

Fujita and his followers at Tsukuba yama became aware of what had taken place, and proposed to unite their efforts with those of Takéda Iga in order to chastise the Wicked Party. There were a number of *rônins* from various provinces among them, who declared as they had taken up arms simply in order to expel the barbarians, they saw no reason why they should concern themselves about the private feuds of the two parties, and they fled from Tsukuba yama in a body. This afforded an opportunity to the Bakufu to kill more than half of them, and

Fujita, finding that so many of his men had deserted, joined Takéda at Naka in the same month with the three hundred men who still remained to him.

When Fujita and his friends first commenced operations, Takéda had regretted the rash and hasty manner in which it had been done, and had hoped to arrange matters. When, therefore, Ichikawa expelled the Righteous Party from the Castle, he proceeded to Mito under the nominal leadership of Matsudaira Ôi no kami, with the object of attempting a solution of the difficulties which had arisen, but Ichikawa resisted him by arms and prevented his entering the Castle. He had consequently occupied the port of Naka and fought every day with Ichikawa, until the latter endeavoured to split up his force by luring away Ôi no kami with fine words. Ôi no kami was about to go and join him, when Takéda remonstrated, saying: "The enemy refuses to admit us, and invites your Lord-"ship alone. His intentions cannot be trusted, and I "secretly entertain fears for your Lordship's safety." Ôi no kami refused to give way to the efforts made to detain him, and proceeded to the town of Mito with a small number of men. Ichikawa reproached him, saying: "Your "Lordship received orders to effect a pacification, and be-"hold! you are in league with rebels." He then made the prince commit suicide, by orders received from the Shôgun, and continued to plot against Takéda. When Takéda heard of what had occurred, he became indignant and said: "The traitorous scoundel has done as I feared." It was then that he accepted the adherence of Fujita, with whom he henceforth acted in concert, thus justifying the accusations of Ichikawa and his friends. Upon this the Bakufu despatched the Drilled Troops, under the command of the Vice-Minister Tanuma Gemba no kami, to chastise Takéda and his companions, and it also ordered the clans of the vicinity, as well as Ichikawa, Asaina and their friends, to render him active aid.

In the 10th month (October 31—November 28) the troops under Takéda and Fujita issued repeatedly from their fastnesses and attacked the forces of the Bakufu. The soldiers of Torii Tamba no kami fought well, and seriously impeded the operations of Takéda, whom the Bakufu's army had now completely surrounded. To add to his difficulties, the provisions began to run short, and some of his men had secret communication with his enemies. The Bakufu therefore made an attack in force, and Takéda, resolving to proceed to Kiôto and make a complaint there, fell upon the besieging force with five hundred men, which were all that remained to him, broke his way through and reached Serata in Kôdzuké. On the night of the 11th December he profited by the darkness to cross the Toné gawa, and found his way on to the Nakasendô. The Bakufu despatched other troops in pursuit and issued orders to all the clans dwelling along that road to chastise him. As he entered the town of Takasaki in the province of Kôdzuké, the local troops turned out to attack him, but were unsuccessful. He then reached the province of Shinano, where he made a vigorous attack on the troops of Matsudaira Tamba no kami and Suwa Inaba no kami, who held the Wada pass, and putting them to flight eventually got into Mino. Having crossed the Kiso gawa at Ota, he bivouacked at Kanô, and was preparing to march west and enter Kiôto, when the troops of Hikoné and Ogaki took up a strong position to his front and barred the road. This forced him to change his route, and in the 12th month [1865] (Dec. 29—Jan. 26) he crossed over the Haibôshi pass into the neighbourhood of Ono in Echizen. The Kaga troops occupied a stockade at Kaidzu in the province of Omi, and Takéda Iga despatched a messenger thither to say that he and his companions had been slandered by Ichikawa and others of the Yûki party, their fellow clansmen, and that having incurred the displeasure of the Bakufu, they wished to find shelter with Shitotsubashi, a relation of their prince, and lay the whole matter before him. This message was also embodied in a letter, asking for permission to pass through Kaidzu, but the Kaga troops refused.

Shitotsubashi Chiunagon, who was at Kiôto, had heard of the approach of Takéda and his followers, and having applied to the Imperial Court for leave to chastise them, marched at the head of some soldiers in the direction of Kaidzu, accompanied by the troops of Odawara, Kuwana, Aidzu, Chikuzen and several other clans. Takéda Iga addressed a letter to him, appealing for pity and consideration, but the Chiunagon would not listen, and wished on the contrary to attack him in force, so as to crush him completely. No resource remained but to seek shelter in Kaga, where it was refused to them. Takéda then addressed a letter, saying : " We are informed that your " clan refuses to admit men who have earned the name of " rebels, and we bow to your decision. We have repeat- " edly resisted the forces of the Bakufu on account of " certain private disputes in our single clan ; we have " broken the august laws of the Empire and cannot atone " for our offences. We do not hope to preserve our lives, " and for that reason we submit to you in a body ; but al- " though we do not expect to live, there is one thing " which still compels us to spend our breath in talking ; " it is the vile name of ' rebels' which has been applied " to us. This is what we cannot bear with equanimity. " We humbly pray you to take these our humble senti- " ments into consideration." In this way they asked that the stigma of rebellion might be removed. The Kaga clan forwarded the letter to the Bakufu, which placed Takéda and his followers in the custody of the local clans. Shitotsubashi then returned to Kiôto. The Bakufu confiscated the lands of Matsudaira Oi no kami and imprisoned his family in one of his *yashiki*. In the following month Takéda and the rest were all decapitated. Four years later the Takéda Party succeeded in taking the lives of Ichikawa and his associates, which event at last put an end " to the dissension of the Righteous and Wicked Parties.

In the autumn of this year certain *rônins* assassinated Sakuma Shôzan in a street at Kiôto. Shôzan had in the year 1854 been condemned to confinement by the authorities of his own clan for complicity in the crime for which Yoshida Shôin was punished, but having been subsequently pardoned, was at this moment residing in the capital. He was constantly employed on business between the Court and the Bakufu, and was a strenuous advocate for the opening of the country to foreigners. He was constantly to be seen mounted on horseback with a saddle and bridle of foreign make, and the hatred which he thus excited in the breasts of those whose object was to expel the barbarians was the cause of the event just mentioned. Common report attributed his murder to some Higo men.

In the same month the ex-Dainagon of Owari, commander-in-chief of the forces sent to chastise Chôshiu, took up his quarters at Hiroshima in the west of Geishiu. He demanded explanations from the House of Môri, and met with an offer of complete submission. Some time before this, those *samurai* of the clan who had abstained from taking part in the attack on Kiôto had taken council together, and had either condemned to domiciliary confinement or to imprisonment Masuda, Fukubara, Kunishi and all those who had shared in the government of the clan at the time of the attack. They had also confined the prince and his son in a temple, thereby offending the general body of their fellow-clansmen, who stigmatized the authors of these measures as the Vulgar View Party (*Zokuron-tô*). The Vulgar View Party retorted by arrest-

---

(46.) The author did not foresee that the feud would break out again in the end of 1872.

ing their traducers and effectually put a stop to the expression of such opinions.

124. Such being the condition of affairs when the invading army appeared on the frontier, the Vulgar View Party destroyed the fences and gates of the batteries placed at the most important strategical points, and barred the doors of every house in the town. They then invited in the officials of the Bakufu, decapitated the three *Karô* and thirteen other prisoners, and delivered up their heads as an atonement for the offences they had been guilty of. These proceedings struck fear into the inhabitants of the town.

125. Owari, the Commander-in-chief, having received the report of the Bakufu's officials, proceeded to pronounce sentence on the five *Kugés* remaining out of the seven who had originally taken refuge in Chôshiu. Of the other two, one had died there, while another had removed to a neighbouring province. The five were placed in the custody of Satsuma, Chikuzen and Higo, and they were forced to give guarantees of sincere contrition for the satisfaction of the Bakufu. In the 1st month of the 1st year of Kei-ô (Jan. 27—Feb. 25) the army was withdrawn to Ozaka, and rumours became current that the expedition against Chôshiu being over, the Shôgun would proceed in person to that city in order to determine the culprit's punishment.

126. During the same month Takasugi Shinsaku took up arms in the territory of the clan, which again became the theatre of commotion. When the Vulgar View Party originally placed the three *Karô* in confinement they had also tried to arrest Shinsaku, who escaped by a miracle and fled to Chikuzen. On hearing that the three *karô* and other members of his party had been put to death, his indignation was extreme. Having returned to Shimonoséki with the intention of ousting the Vulgar View Party, and restoring the previous state of things, he despatched

messengers to all parts to summon troops to his aid. So
far back as 1863, when the House of Môri began to plan
the expulsion of the barbarians, Shinsaku had arrived at
the conclusion that the luxurious *samurai* class was of no
practical value in the field, and he obtained permission
from the authorities of the clan to organize troops on a
new system. This consisted in breaking through the
prejudice which existed in favour of birth, in selecting
strong able-bodied men from the common people as well as
from the *samurai* class, and in fixing the pay of the
battalions which he thus formed at a high rate. The
strictest discipline was enforced, and even the most
ruffianly vagabonds willingly obeyed him. His troops
were bold and valiant in fight, and went by the name of
Kiheitai, or the "Irregular Troops." In the execution of
these measures he was aided chiefly by Iriyé Kuichi and
Kuzaka Gisuké, and the old abuses were rapidly reformed.
The whole clan caught the infection, and large numbers
enrolling themselves, raised Shinsaku, Kuzaka and Iriyé to
the command. Kuzaka and Iriyé, however, had fallen at
Kiôto, and when Shinsaku fled to Chikuzen the men dispersed into hiding: No sooner did they hear of his proclamation than five hundred men came flocking to join
him. Having taken counsel with Ôta Ichinoshin, Yamagata Kiôsuké and others, Shinsaku attacked the government offices at Shimonoséki, seized all the ammunition
he could find, and ordered the rich merchants of the town
to supply him with money. Having collected a large
quantity of provisions and arms, he next prepared to attack
the castle of Hagi at the head of his troops.

The Vulgar View Party were terribly alarmed, and reported the outbreak of the insurrection to the Bakufu, and
carrying the prince and his son into the castle, sent orders
throughout the two provinces for the speedy chastisement
of the rebels. The common people were also forbidden to
sell food or clothing to the Irregular Troops, and finally a

Karô named Awaya took command of the forces and marched to attack them. The Irregular Troops anticipated him, and inflicted a severe defeat upon the Vulgar View party, who thereupon brought more men into the field, and continued the fight for three whole days, but being finally worsted, were compelled to retreat and defend the castle of Hagi. Here they were immediately surrounded by the victorious Irregulars, who were on the point of taking the place by storm, when peace was arranged through the medium of a third party. Takasugi and his friends decapitated the chiefs of the Vulgar View Party and pilloried their heads in the camp. From this moment dissension ceased, and the whole clan worked for one common object. Takasugi and his friends carried off the prince and his son to Yamaguchi in Suwô, where extensive fortifications had been constructed in the year when the expulsion of the barbarians was first resolved upon. The two princes had been originally removed to this stronghold, but after the attack on Kiôto the Vulgar View Party had placed them in a temple at Hagi, and they were now carried back again.

Having thus far been successful, Takasugi and his friends took counsel. It was evident that the objects aimed at by the Bakufu in attempting to punish the clan would not be satisfied by the execution of the three *karô*, and besides it was certain to make a fresh attack as soon as it became acquainted with the recent proceedings. The only course left was to make a determined resistance, and if necessary, by laying down their lives, to soothe the souls of those who had preceded them in death. These ideas being communicated to their followers were received with universal enthusiasm.

In the fight at Kiôto it was the valour of the Satsuma clan which led to the defeat of the Chôshiu men, a large number of whom had fallen into its hands. But the Satsuma men now began to regret the course which they had taken on that occasion. In face of passing events, idly to fight amongst themselves, and to wrangle over petty matters was a bad policy for the Japanese. It seemed much better that the Government of the country should be conducted from one centre, and that the nation should be united for the defence of the empire. They therefore treated the prisoners with great kindness, and loading them with presents, sent them back to Chôshiu. When the occurrences just related took place, Saigô Kichinosuké sent a secret messenger to Chôshiu to negotiate a common understanding between the two clans. The Chôshiu men deliberated together; they felt that of course victory could not be hoped for in a contest in which all the available forces of the Empire were ranged against an isolated fortress, but that all they could expect was, when their strength was finally exhausted, to perish with their household gods. If in a critical moment like this, when their existence hung but by a hair, they were to enter into relations with another clan, posterity would condemn them as cowards. Some, who acknowledged the justice of these arguments, were yet of opinon that to reject such a magnanimous offer as that of the Satsuma clan might seem ungracious. Besides it was not impossible that with such aid they might be enabled to preserve their own clan from destruction. It happened that a Tosa man, named Sakamoto Riôma, who was in Chôshiu at this moment, supported these views, and his advice being followed, the enmity of the two clans was henceforth at an end.

130 Saigô had spent the time between 1854 and 1859 in Kiôto and Ôzaka. Being much dissatisfied with the course things were taking, and possessing definite views of his own, he gradually formed a party, but when Ii Kamon no kami came into power he returned to his native province. During his residence in Kiôto he had become intimate with a bonze of the monastery called Jôjiu-In, named Gas-

shô, a man of patriotic views. In the year 1858, when all the men of spirit in various parts of the country were arrested, Gasshô was also captured, but succeeded in making his escape and fled to Satsuma, where he found concealment in Saigô's house. Having explained to the latter the state of things at Kiôto, he said: "Seeing that matters have come to this pass, and that we shall all be killed, rather than die by the hand of some traitor, it is better to jump into the sea and make an end of ourselves." Saigô agreeing, they went secretly by night and threw themselves into the sea. Fortunately it was a moonlight night and a boat was just passing the spot. The boatmen, seeing what had occurred, saved them, and finding both to be perfectly insensible, applied all the remedies in their power. Saigô was recalled to life with great difficulty, but Gasshô was a corpse."[47] When the Satsuma authorities heard of this they exiled Saigô to Ôshima, fearing the comments of the Bakufu. Before this Saigô had already been twice banished to Ôshima for some reason or another, and he now changed his name to Ôshima Sanyémon, in allusion to his having visited that island three times. As a special favour he was afterwards allowed by the authorities of the clain to return home, and at the time when he sent the envoy to Chôshiu he appears to have had a great share in the direction of affairs in Satsuma.

[131] The Court and the Bakufu were as yet ignorant that Satsuma and Chôshiu had entered into relations, and the former, hearing of the outbreak in Chôshiu, sent repeated orders to the Shôgun to proceed to Kiôto. In the 4th month (April 25—May 24) the Shôgun again proclaimed his intention of chastising Chôshiu throughout the empire, and the points where the two provinces of Nagato and Suwô were to be attacked were definitely mapped out.

---

(47) This account is not quite correct. Saigô and the bonze were being conveyed across the bay from Kagoshima to Sakurajima in a boat under guard, and profiting by the inattention of their conductors jumped overboard. They were picked up by the boatmen, but the bonze was saved last.

The Shôgun was himself to take the field at the head of
all his vassals, and the troops were frequently exercised
before him on the parade ground which had been formed
at Komabagahara (near Yedo).

The ex-Dainagon of Owari had written a letter in the
5th month (May 25—June 22), to the Shôgun, as soon as
he had heard of the affair, saying:—" Last year I report-
" ed that Chôshiu had made atonement by inflicting capit-
" al punishment on his chief retainers, and yet your High-
" ness is preparing to take the field in person against him.
" I confess I see no adequate reason for this course, for if
" he was justly accused of any crime, the whole Empire
" would declare that he ought to be chastised, and would
" march against him. It is not right wantonly to take
" up arms without manifest cause. Besides the very exist-
" ence of the Tokugawa family depends on the result, and I
" pray your Highness therefore to give this matter your
" profoundest consideration before proceeding to act." The
Shôgun was deaf to these remonstrances. Katsu Awa no
kami also maintained that there was no just cause for
going to war, to the great displeasure of the Shôgun's
ministers, who suspected him of being in Chôshiu's interest, and dismissed him from office.

In the intercalary 5th month (June 23—July 22) the
Shôgun eventually started from Yedo by the Tôkaidô,
and had an audience of the Mikado on the day following
his arrival at Kiôto. He then proceeded at once to
Ôzaka. The troops of the dependent *daimiôs* and the *ha-
tamotos* advanced by the Tôkaidô about the same time,
but their march was greatly impeded by the swollen condition of the rivers consequent upon the heavy rains
which had fallen. The post-towns were crowded with
troops, and the last who left Yedo did not arrive in
Ôzaka until fifty-three days after the Shôgun.

In the 6th month (November 18—December 17)[48] the

---

(48) The dates given are all incorrect. The English, French and

foreign representatives resident at Yokohama prepared to proceed to Ôzaka with the object of presenting a request to the Shôgun. The Ministers, who were alarmed at the prospect of their presenting themselves in the vicinity of the Imperial capital, endeavoured to dissuade them, but the representatives declined to listen, and finally arrived at Hiôgo, whence they forwarded their letter. Shitotsubashi Chiunnagon, Aidzu Chiujô, Ogasawara Jijiu and others thereupon addressed a joint memorial to the Court, saying: "The foreigners have come up to the Home
" Provinces to request that your Majesty will signify
" your consent to the Treaties and to demand the opening
" of Hiôgo. They say that they have come to arrange
" these matters directly with Your Majesty, as the Bakufu
" is unable to settle them. Your servants will do all in their
" power to create delays, but unless the Imperial consent
" to the Treaties is given, the foreigners will not quit the
" Inland Sea. If we were lightly to use force against
" them, we might be victorious for the moment, but a
" tiny piece of territory like this could not long withstand
" the combined armies of the universe. We are not so
" much concerned for the preservation of the Bakufu as
" for the security of the throne. If the result be what
" we must anticipate, your people will be plunged into
" the depths of misery. Your Majesty's sacred wish of
" protecting and succouring your subjects will be render-
" ed unavailing, and the Bakufu will be unable to fulfil
" its mission, which is to govern the country happily.
" Your servants cannot find heart to obey Your Majesty's

Dutch squadrons left Yokohama on Nov. 1, carrying the English, French and Dutch Ministers and the American Chargé d'Affaires, and arrived at Hiôgo on the 4th. Negotiations were commenced on the following day, and were terminated on the 24th by a letter from the ministers of the Shôgun, in which they enclosed a copy of the decree announcing the Mikado's general consent to the Treaties. With characteristic duplicity they omitted from this copy the postcript in which the opening of Hiôgo was forbidden and a revision of the Treaties also commanded. As there is no article in the Japanese language the omission of these two conditions made it appear that the Mikado had given his consent to the Treaties as they then stood, which was not his intention.

"order to break off foreign relations, and humbly pray
"that Your Majesty, deigning to take these things into
"consideration, will at once give your consent." The
Court debated over the matter, and after having carefully
weighed the political state, sent the two Tensô Asukai
and Nonomiya to communicate His Majesty's consent to
the Bakufu on the 30th November, ordering it at the
same time to revise the hitherto existing Treaties. At
the same time the opening of the port of Hiôgo was prohibited. It is said that this last order was given because
the Satsuma clan had shortly before addressed a memorial
to the Court remonstrating against the opening of Hiôgo.
From the time when the Bakufu first concluded Treaties
in 1855 the whole country had been constantly discussing
the matter with great eagerness, but the Imperial consent
was now obtained for the first time.

The Shôgun, who felt severely the weight of domestic
and foreign affairs, about this time sent in a memorial to
the Mikado praying for leave to resign his office to Shitotsubashi Chiunagon, on the ground of ill-health. The
Imperial Court expressed great sympathy for him, but
refused his request, and urged him to settle the Chôshiu
affair without delay.

1866. In the 12th month (Jan. 17—Feb. 14) the
Bakufu sent orders for a Chôshiu *Karô* to come up to
Ôzaka, and Shishido Bingo no suké came in obedience to
the summons as far as Hiroshima in Geishiu, where the
Bakufu reproached him with the equivocal appearance
which the late conduct of the House of Môri presented.
Bingo no suké gave full explanations, which nevertheless
did not remove the suspicions of the Bakufu officials, who
arrested him and placed him in the custody of the prince
of Geishiu. The Bakufu about this time despatched the
Drilled Troops and the troops of the various clans to the
western frontier of Geishiu, with the object of taking measures against Chôshiu, and they remained there in their
quarters without moving until the beginning of spring.

136 In the 4th month (May 15—June 12) a report coming to the Chôshiu troops quartered in the south of Suwô that the eastern forces were lying inactive in Geishiu, a hundred and fifty men, disregarding orders, secretly left Chôshiu, and seized Kurashiki in Bitchiu, but the Bakufu's men in Geishiu, hastening to the spot, attacked the band at Abékawa in the vicinity and put it to flight.

137 Orders had previously been issued by the Bakufu to all the clans, directing them to bring their troops into the field, but the Satsuma clan now sent in a memorial, protesting against the injustice of the war, and declining to furnish its quota.

138 The *Samurai* of the Chôshiu clan had sent a letter to Geishiu, saying: "Since the prince and his son gave "undoubted proofs of contrition in the winter of the "year before last all the clans have been expecting to "see the Bakufu behave with leniency towards them, "but troops are daily arriving in your territory. This "causes great anxiety and excitement throughout our "clan, and a hundred and fifty men who were encamped "in the southern part of the territory secretly deserted "on the 16th of May, with arms in their hands, and we "do not know what has become of them, except that "they went away by sea. It is not impossible that, "believing false rumours, they may commit violent "acts in a fit of desperation, for which the clan "would be held responsible. We beg you, therefore, to "arrest them, should they enter the limits of your juris- "diction. Please at the same time to communicate the "contents of this letter to the Bakufu." Hereupon the Bakufu at last issued its commands to the House of Môri, saying: "Although you have shown evidence of a sub- "missive temper by inflicting capital punishment on your "*karôs* and their advisers, and by confining yourselves "within the walls of a monastery, you must be held re- "sponsible for having lost the art of ruling your retain-

"ers. Permission has therefore been obtained from the
"Imperial Court to inflict three additional penalties on
"you, namely, the forfeiture of one hundred thousand
"*koku* of land, the perpetual confinement of the chief of
"the clan and his son, leaving the succession to your eldest
"grandson, and the extinction of the families of the three
"*karôs.*" A day was fixed for the answer to be sent in.
The indignation of the clan knew no bounds. It was
resolved to await the attack of the Bakufu and to try the
issue of a resort to arms, and they purposely delayed
answering in order to gain more time for their preparations.

The Bakufu had established its headquarters at Hiroshima in Geishiu, under the prince of Kishiu, Commander-in-Chief, and Ogasawara Iki no kami, Lieut. General of the forces, who issued their orders to the other divisions from this place. After waiting thirty days, and finding that no answer came, they decided that the judgment had been treated with contempt, and applied to the Imperial Court for leave to attack. The Imperial Court in reply bade them do their duty with all speed.

In the 6th month (July 12—Aug. 9) therefore, the Bakufu at last sent troops to attack Nagato and Suwô on all sides. The drilled troops, in conjunction with the troops of Kishiu, Hikoné, Takata and a naval division, advanced on the Geishiu side. The troops of Tottori, Matsué, Hamada, Fukuyama and some of Kishiu advanced by way of Iwami (or Sékishiu). Those of Higo, Yanagawa and Kokura, with another naval division were to act from Buzen (on the opposite side of the Shimonoséki Strait), while a detachment of the drilled troops and the Matsuyama troops attacked the island of Ôshima.

On the 13th July Ogasawara Iki no kami proceeded to Kokura to direct the operations of the Buzen column.

On the 19th Kôno Toda and some others arrived at Ôshima with a force composed of fifteen hundred infantry and the Matsuyama troops, all embarked in large vessels, and bombarded the shore, setting fire to the villages. The Chôshiu forces not replying, the eastern troops landed, attacked the Chôshiu barracks on the morning of the 23rd, and took them by assault. Takasugi Shinsaku and Yamagata Kiôsuké, commanding in Chôshiu, on hearing of the attack, despatched fighting vessels against the eastern troops, and the losses were about equal on either side.

143 On the 26th the Chôshiu forces invited an encounter by sending out a small body of men, who being attacked by the eastern troops, took to flight, and led them, flushed with victory, into the midst of an ambuscade. They were speedily routed, and throwing away their arms, took refuge on board the ships. Sakuma Ikkaku, a Matsuyama leader, was killed on this occasion. At midnight the Easterners collected their defeated men, and returned to Geishiu. The Chôshiu men laughed scornfully at the cowardice of the Eastern troops, and said they were not worth contending with.

144 The Geishiu column advanced by sea and land, and the vanguard, composed of Hikoné and Takata troops, prepared to cross the frontier. It had been resolved on the Chôshiu side to anticipate the attack, and, accordingly, Ôta Ichinoshin and Ishikawa Kogorô, at the head of eight hundred men, quietly crossed the upper waters of the Oségawa, and attacked the eastern army in the rear, while at the same time they despatched another detachment to engage its vanguard. The battle thus began in front and rear at the same moment, and the eastern army after suffering a severe defeat, fled, the men throwing away their muskets and abandoning their artillery. The Chôshiu men followed up their victory by entering the Geishin territory, where they occupied Ôtaké, Ogata and Kuwa, having Shijiuhassaka between themselves and the enemy, who retreated and encamped at Ôno.

145 The eastern forces in Iwami had fixed on a day for

making an attack by several roads, when the Chôshiu commanders Inouyé Bunda and Ômura Masujirô made an irruption into the Hamada territory at the head of twelve hundred men. The Matsué and Hadama troops had taken up a position on Mounts Hibari and Taëma, where they resisted the attack, but the Chôshiu troops made a circuit to their rear and encamped at the foot of the hills. The Matsué men then ascended to the summit, and poured down such a fire that the Chôshiu leaders were put to flight, but again putting their men in motion, they climbed mount Taëma, and attacked the Hamada camp with skirmishers. The Hamada troops being unable to withstand the assault, abandoned the place and fled. Having thus obtained possession of Mount Taëma, they took the Matsué troops on Mount Hibari in flank, who after a vigorous but ineffectual resistance were compelled to retreat to the town of Hamada.

146 At this moment another division, composed of Hamada and Fukuyama troops, about sixteen hundred in number, was lying at Masuda. On the 28th July a thousand Chôshiu men, taking advantage of the morning mist, surprised it in front and rear, and routed it most effectually. Yamamoto Hanya, a Hamada leader, fell on this occasion. The Chôshiu forces retook Masuda, seized all the provisions in the place, crossed the river Sufugawa and attacked the town of Hamada. The troops of Kishiu, Matsuó, Fukuyama, Hamada, and other clans, who were stationed in the vicinity, offered a vigorous resistance, but were thrown into disorder after several skirmishes, losing an officer of rank named Mieda Giôbu.

147 The Chôshiu troops attacked Hamada on the following day, and the garrison, knowing their own inability to resist, set fire to the place and retreated. The Prince and his family fled to Idzumo by sea, and the whole of the eastern forces having retired into Geishiu, the Chôshiu men advanced and seized the government buildings of the

collectorate of Ômori. With this operation the subjugation of the province of Iwami by the arms of Chôshiu was completed.

148   The commander of the Kokura division also prepared about this time to attack Shimonoséki, whereupon Takasugi, Yamagata and other Chôshiu leaders gave orders for three large vessels to attack Tanoüra (on the south side of the strait), and a party having been landed, an engagement took place with thirteen hundred picked Kokura troops commanded by Shimamura Shima. The Chôshiu men maintained the struggle from eight o'clock in the morning until four in the afternoon, but getting the worst of it, burnt the village and retired, carrying off the arms they had found there.

149   Shortly before this a French man-of-war had called at Shimonoséki on its way from Yokohama to Nagasaki to inform the Chôshiu people that their nation had entered into an alliance with the Japanese Government, and that if Chôshiu refused to obey the orders of the latter, they, the French, would be compelled to assist their ally. They therefore recommended Chôshiu to submit. They also gave notice that they would return from Nagasaki in ten days for an answer. Having delivered a letter to this effect the vessel proceeded on its voyage.

150   The Chôshiu men deliberated, saying: "Why should "we accept dictation from foreign countries in our inter-"nal affairs? We had better proceed to take active mea-"sures before the Frenchmen arrive." They therefore ravaged the domain of Kokura with fire, and when the French came a second time, and reproached them, they replied: "The Bakufu has ravaged the island of Ôshima "which belongs to us, and has burnt the villages, killing "all the innocent inhabitants. Besides, the Kokura clan "has for a long time not acted as neighbours should. "Further, the eastern army is stationed in their territory, "and is ready to attack us at any moment. What obliga-

"tion compels us to sit down quietly and await its onset?"
It happened that an English vessel turned up at this
moment, and the commander having effected a reconciliation by his good offices, the Frenchmen at last departed.
It was said that they had been to Nagasaki on a secret
errand for the Bakufu.

151   On the 30th of July, the Drilled Troops and the troops
of Ôgaki and Kishiu being encamped at Ôno, the Chôshiu
troops advanced over Shijiuhassaka in a direct line, at six
o'clock in the morning, and from Matsugahara against the
enemy's flank, and profiting by the mist surprised Ôno.
The eastern forces defended themselves vigorously, and
the bullets fell as thick as hail. About ten o'clock the
Chôshiu troops were defeated and forced to retreat, with
very heavy losses, to Kuwa, where they halted.

152   Before dawn on the 5th of August the Chôshiu forces
again crossed Shijiuhassaka and attacked the Eastern
camp. The Easterners bombarded their rear with their
men-of-war, and scattered them. At this moment another
detachment was advancing from Takinokuchi by a bye-
path, and encountered an united volley fired by the Easterners from the top of a hill, but attacking the hill with
skirmishers, who fired as they climbed, they succeeded
in dislodging them. Then bringing their field artillery into play, they directed their fire upon the enemy
in the valley below, throwing him into great confusion.
Profiting by this success they made a direct attack on the
camp, where a fierce combat ensued. At noon, neither side
having gained the advantage, they discontinued firing, the
Easterners retreating to Ôno. In this battle both sides
fought with desperation, and lost so many men in killed
and wounded that the fields were covered with corpses.

153   Shortly before this, Matsudaira Hôki no kami, who had
replaced Ogasawara Iki no kami at Hiroshima, set Shishido
Bingo no suké at liberty and sent him back to Chôshiu.
This act was regarded by the prince of Kishiu, who was

commander-in-chief, as highly calculated to obstruct the success of the operations, and in his anger he reported it to Ôzaka. The Bakufu consequently summoned Hôki no kami to Ôzaka, and reprimanded him for his bad conduct. Hôki no kami endeavoured to exculpate himself, saying: "When your servant was at Hiroshima, he heard that "the Satsuma clan had secret relations with the enemy, "and that a large number of Chôshiu men hidden in the "three capital cities, were continually spying out the state "of our affairs. We are unable therefore to conceal the "facts from them. Besides the English were secretly "selling ships and gunpowder to the enemy, who were "gaining strength every day. With the object of under- "mining their strength, your servant therefore took the "resolution of confiding his private opinion to Bingo no "suké, whom he sent back." Having sent in a letter to this effect, he awaited his punishment.

154 On the 6th of September the Eastern forces again arrived at Ôno, and daily councils were held as to the means of making a general attack on Chôshiu by sea and land.

155 The Chôshiu forces had at this moment seized Dairi and Tonoüra in Buzen, where they constructed batteries, and then engaged the Higo and Kokura troops with three hundred men, which was the whole number at their disposal. The Kokura troops having been frequently defeated, thirteen hundred Higo men engaged the enemy at Akazaka and routed him, with a loss of one hundred men. When the news was brought to Chôshiu, fresh troops were despatched from Shimonoséki, and with this reinforcement a series of engagements was fought, until at sunset both combatants retired from the field, the Chôshiu forces encamping at Dairi.

156 Ogasawara Iki no kami having been unsuccessful on several occasions, Higo and Yanagawa withdrew their troops, and Iki no kami, hastily embarking in a man-of-war, fled to Nagasaki. The Chôshiu forces profited by

the lucky turn affairs had taken to attack Kokura with vigour, and its defendants, being now entirely unsupported, burnt the castle on the 9th of September, and retreated to Kaharu.

The eastern army at Ôno crossed the pass of Shijiuhassaka on the 10th September, and the land and sea forces advancing in concert attacked the enemy at Kuwa and Obata. The latter came forth to give battle, and the noise of artillery resounded on all sides, causing the hills to roll down into the valleys. It happened that rain had been falling for several days, and the roads were everywhere so muddy that both combatants were much impeded in their movements. After an engagement which lasted from ten o'clock a.m. to four o'clock p.m. the left wing of the eastern army was broken, and the Chôshiu men made an attack with all their available force, to which the enemy succumbing, burnt the village of Kuwa and retreated. At the same moment the troops of Takata, Hikoné and Kishiu were engaging the Chôshiu forces at Matsugahara and Kunai, but being defeated with great loss, they had to retreat to Ôno.

On the 16th of September the Chôshiu forces, divided into three columns, surprised Ôno under cover of a storm of wind and rain, and invited a battle with their musketeers, but the eastern army, which had not recovered from the panic caused by its defeat of the previous day, did not accept the challenge, and finally retreated to Hiroshima. The Chôshiu troops at once pursued it, and after taking Ôno advanced upon Hiroshima.

In this campaign the eastern troops wore armour and surcoats, and their weapons were swords and spears, while the Chôshiu men, clad in light, short-sleeved garments, and dispensing with their swords, were chiefly armed with muskets. Their drill, too, was excellent. In fact the Chôshiu clan had gained a great deal of experience in the year 1863, which they had turned to account in remodelling their military system. This enabled them on each occasion to beat the eastern army, which at no period was able to gain a footing on the Chôshiu territory.

160 Some time before this the Shôgun fell ill, and a messenger was sent to Ôzaka by the Mikado to inquire after his health.

161 The Imperial Court then ordered Shitotsubashi Chiunagon to take the direction of the forces in the Shôgun's stead, and he was on the point of setting off for Geishiu when the news of the last defeat arrived at Kiôto and Ôzaka. The clans who had joined the expedition at once withdrew their troops, and the whole country was in a state of alarm, not knowing what would come next. The Shôgun was agitated by constant anxiety, and on the 19th September he died at Ôzaka. Hereupon Shitotsubashi Chiunagon began to regret his previous willingness to obey the Mikado's will, and consequently sent in a memorial in which he took blame to himself for having committed this error, and declined to proceed to Geishiu. He also requested leave to assemble all the Princes who had supported him at Kiôto, in order to deliberate on the state of affairs. The Imperial Court having given its sanction to his proposal, the Chiunagon himself drew up a circular, summoning the ex-Dainagon of Owari, Matsudaira Shimotsuké no kami (eldest son of the Prince of Chikuzen), Matsudaira Kansô (ex-Prince of Hizen), Matsudaira Yôdô (ex-Prince of Tosa), Daté Tôtômi no kami (ex-Prince of Uwajima in Iyo), Shimadzu Ôsumi no kami (father of the Prince of Satsuma) and Nagaöka Riônoské (younger brother of the Prince of Higo).

162 On the 3rd October the Imperial Court gave orders for the operations against Chôshiu to be discontinued, pretexting the death of the Shôgun, which orders were notified to all the clans by the Bakufu.

163 In the course of the month the Imperial Court conferred

the succession to the headship of the Tokugawa family upon Shitotsubashi Chiunagon.

At this very time the Chôshiu forces were encamped before Hiroshima in Geishiu, and their garrison at Kokura continually harassed the troops of that clan, the cause of their hostility being the quarrel which had lasted since first the Chôshiu men began to expel the barbarians. The Kokura clan laid its griefs before the two clans of Satsuma and Higo, who thereupon sent an envoy to Chôshiu to effect a reconciliation. The latter demanded an oath in writing from the Kokura clan that they would lay down their arms, which was signed by the prince and all his family. The Chôshiu clan notified this to the garrison in Buzen, and peace was restored.

In the course of the same month the Bakufu, recognizing the high estimation in which Katsu Awa no kami was held by all the clans, sent him to Geishiu, to offer terms to Chôshiu and to withdraw the troops. He was received in conference by Hirozawa Hiôské and Inouyé Bunda, and communicated to them the will of the Mikado and the orders of the Shôgun. The Chôshiu forces were ordered to return home, but the men were angry and refused to obey. The two commanders, unwilling to disregard the Shôgun's order and grateful for the courtesy of Awa no kami, succeeded in pacifying them, and they returned in great triumph to their native province after five days had elapsed.

The war was now over at last. During its continuance the Bakufu had expended vast sums of money until its treasuries were almost exhausted, and yet it was unable to have its way with Chôshiu. From this time onwards the great clans neglected to obey the commands of Bakufu, and its power eventually decayed.

1867.—On the 6th of January 1867, the Imperial Court offered the appointment of Shôgun to Shitotsubashi Chiunagon. He repeatedly declined it, but the Court, while addressing him most graciously, insisted on his acceptance of it, and he found himself compelled at last to give way. The Mikado's envoy then proceeded to the castle of Nijô (at Kiôto, not far from the Palace) and invested him with the office.

On the 3rd of February the Emperor Kômei Tennô died, and was succeeded by the heir-apparent, who is the reigning sovereign.

In the early part of the year the Bakufu obtained some Frenchmen to instruct the infantry, cavalry and artillery.

In the course of the summer riots occurred among the peasantry of Kôshiu and Shinshiu, but the Bakufu despatched the drilled troops against them and order was speedily restored.

In the autumn Enomoto Kamajirô and his companions came back to Japan from Holland on board the *Kaiyô-maru*.

About the same time the Bakufu despatched envoys to Russia to treat about the boundary in Sagalien. In 1862 Takénoüchi Shimotsuké no kami and Matsudaira Iwami no kami had been previously sent thither to discuss the same question. They proposed on that occasion to fix on the fiftieth parallel of latitude as the boundary, because it marked the division between the tribes called Aino and Smelenkur. Our officers were to proceed thither to govern the natives, and a map was prepared in which the respective territories were coloured red and green, the fiftieth parallel of latitude lying between the two. The Russians replied: " On what grounds do you call this your " territory? If we were to consult an impartial person he " would decide that the island belonged to Manchuria. " Besides, no Ainos are to be found north of the fortieth " parallel, and you have quite disregarded the position of " the tribes in your unjustifiable desire to take the fiftieth " parallel as a boundary. How is it possible for us to ac- " cept this? There is nothing in this island by which a

"boundary can be properly laid down, and under these
"circumstances, if you insist upon laying one down, it
"will give rise to complications between the two powers.
"We are naturally averse to having our frontier undefin-
"ed, but we are equally averse to defining it on insuf-
"ficient grounds, or on such as do not suit our con-
"venience. Let us, therefore, leave the matter as it is for
"the present, permitting our respective subjects to occupy
"the island in common, as was provisionably determined
"by the treaty concluded with Japan at Shimoda. At
"some future day, when we have both examined the
"localities, we can confer again. But if you still find it
"absolutely necessary to settle something, we will take
"Aniwa Bay (at the extreme south of Sagalien) as our
"boundary." Although Takénoüchi and his colleagues
perceived from the evasive nature of their arguments that
their design was to seize the whole island, they were
unable to refute the reasoning of the Russians because
they were insufficiently acquainted with the nature of the
locality.

173 An engagement having been entered into in writing to
the effect that the discussion should be renewed on the
basis of an examination of the localities, the envoys returned to Japan, reported the evident desire of the Russians to make themselves possessors of the whole island,
and requested that some person who was well acquainted
with the geography of the island should be sent to negotiate. The Bakufu, although desirous of despatching a
second mission, had so much on its hands during the
five years which followed that it was unable to carry
out its intention, and the Russians took advantage of
this long interval to form extensive settlements in Sagalien. When the Bakufu became aware of their proceedings, it was highly alarmed, and forthwith despatched
Koidé Yamato no kami (Governor of Hakodaté) and
Ishikawa Kawachi no kami (a commissioner for foreign

affairs). On arriving at St. Petersburg, Koidé produced the agreement made by Takénoüchi and his colleagues in 1862, and proposed to discuss the question on the basis of the nature of the localities. The Russians feigned never to have heard of the arrangement, and offered in exchange for Sagalien certain of the Kurile Islands, which belonged to them, but Koidé and his colleagues denied their jurisdiction over the Kuriles, and upbraided them for their disingenuousness. The argument became warm, until the Russians at last said : " It is not a matter about " which we ought to wrangle. Let us both colonize and " occupy it." Koidé and his colleague consulted together, saying : " Though we have exhausted all possible argu-" ments, the fact remains that their colonies extend south " of the fiftieth parallel. It is our fault for putting the " negotiation off so long." Eventually they made a convention by which the island was to be occupied jointly by Russian and Japanese subjects, and returned home in the following spring to report the result of their mission.

In the 4th month (May 4—June 2) Daté Iyo no kami and Shimadzu Ôsumi no kami arrived at Kiôto, where they were shortly afterwards joined by Matsudaira Shungaku (ex-Prince of Echizen), Nabéshima Kansô (ex-Prince of Hizen) and Yamanoüchi Yôdô (ex-Prince of Tosa [49]).

Shortly before this the representatives of the foreign powers had come to Hiôgo to congratulate the Shôgun upon his succession, and to make certain requests of him. He invited them to an interview at Ôzaka. The foreign representatives then urged the speedy opening of Hiôgo, and the Shôgun consequently addressed a memorial to the Mikado, saying : " Although the date originally fixed " for the opening of Hiôgo has now been exceeded by two " years, your servants were able to put the foreigners

---

(49) These are the same persons as those mentioned as being summoned by the new Shôgun. The author has anticipated events in making them here resume their proper surnames, as that change was not made until after the revolution of 1868.

"off, by alleging the disturbed state of the country,
"but now they have come to press for the perform-
"ance of the promise. Among the numerous nations
"of which the universe outside Japan is composed,
"for fear the strong should oppress the weak, it is the
"custom to enter into treaties according to which the in-
"tercourse of great and small is regulated and good faith
"observed. Such weighty matters are treaties. There-
"fore, even though they come to Hiôgo, your servant can
"ensure that they do not treat us in an overbearing man-
"ner. Besides, the opening of Hiôgo is stipulated in the
"treaties, and we cannot break our word. I pray, there-
"fore, that the Imperial Court will give its consent."
The Imperial Court consulted the clans, most of whom
signified their approval, and it accorded its consent in the
month of June.

176 In the 6th month (July 2—30) a rich merchant of
Ôzaka, named Yamanaka Zenyémon, was chosen with
nineteen others to form a trading corporation (*Shôsha*);
annual grants of rice were made to them, and they were
privileged to wear swords. This was done in view of
the opening of Hiôgo.

177 In the course of the same month the Bakufu, finding its
coffers empty, proposed to issue paper money.

178 Although the Bakufu still continued to carry on the government, it usually referred all matters of importance to the
Imperial Court for decision. Shimadzu Ôsumi no kami
and the other five princes remained at Kiôto, but Yamanoüchi Yôdô returned to his native province on account of
serious ill health. In the 9th month (Sept. 28—Oct. 26),
after he had for some time secretly grieved over the
troubled state of the country, he addressed a letter from
Tosa to the Shôgun, advising him to restore the whole
governing power to the Imperial Court. The letter said:
"It appears to me that although the government and the
"penal laws have been administered by the Military Class

"ever since the middle ages, yet, from the arrival of
"foreigners we have been squabbling amongst ourselves,
"and much public discussion has been excited. The east-
"and west have risen in arms against each other, and
"civil war has never ceased, the effect being to draw on
"us the insult of foreign nations. The cause of this lies
"in the fact that the administration proceeds from two
"centres, causing the Empire's ears and eyes to be turn-
"ed in two different directions. The march of events has
"brought about a revolution, and the old system can no
"longer be obstinately persevered in. You should re-
"store the governing power into the hands of the sovereign,
"and so lay a foundation on which Japan may take its
"stand as the equal of all other countries. This is the
"most imperative duty of the present moment, and is the
"heartfelt prayer of Yôdô. Your Highness is wise
"enough to take this advice into consideration." He then
despatched his retainers Terauchi Sazen and Gotô Shôjirô
to advise the Shôgun to resign the reins of power. The
Shôgun from this time frequently summoned Gotô and
Komatsu of the Satsuma clan to his castle of Nijô to discuss politics with perfect freedom, and both of them per-
sistently advocated the formation of an imperial Government.

The Shôgun became convinced of its expediency, and
drew up a document for communication to his vassals. It
said: "When I contemplate the changes which have
"come about in the political condition of the Empire, it
"appears to me that when the imperial authority decayed
"many centuries back, the power was seized by the Fuji-
"wara family. During the wars of Hôgen and Heiji
"(1156-1159) it passed into the grasp of the Military
"Class. My ancestor was a recipient of especial favours
"at the hands of the Emperor, and during over two hund-
"red years his descendants have enjoyed the same favours
"successively. Although I hold my ancestor's office, there

"has been great mal-administration of the government and
"of the penal laws, the result being the present state of
"affairs. This is the effect of my want of virtue and I can-
"not sufficiently deplore it. It appears to me that the laws
"cannot be maintained in face of the daily extension of
"our foreign relations, unless the government be conducted
"by one head, and I propose therefore to surrender the
"whole governing power into the hands of the Imperial
"Court. This is the best I can do for the interests of the
"Empire in this moment, and I call upon you all to give
"your opinion as to the advisability of this course." Although none of the *samurai* made any open opposition, some of them were secretly dissatisfied.

On the 19th of November, the Shôgun eventually sent in a memorial offering his resignation to the Mikado. This was accepted in considerate language, and he was informed that he was desired to carry on the administration as heretofore, with the exception of directing the actions of the *daimiôs*, which question would be decided as soon as the prince of Kaga and thirty-three other great princes should arrive at Kiôto. A proclamation was then issued throughout the country notifying the Shôgun's resignation of the governing power. The princes who were under obligations to the Tokugawa family advised the Imperial Court not to take the direction of affairs upon its shoulders without due consideration, and the Court began to feel distrust in its own capacity. It was said by some people that a secret understanding existed between Tokugawa Naifu (the ex-Shôgun), the In no Miya and the Kuambaku, that his retainers were acting in concert with the latter, and that the vacillation of the Court was due to these causes. Hereupon the Court nobles and the *samurai* of Satsuma, Tosa and other clans, who had been agitating for a return to the ancient régime of the Mikados, said to themselves: "See how the Court conducts itself,
"at the very moment when the affairs of the Empire seem

"on the point of being settled. The opportunity will "be lost." They proceeded to infuse their vehement opinions into the councils of the Court, which began to bestir itself.

1868.—On the 3rd of January 1868, an order was suddenly issued by the Imperial Court, dismissing the Aidzu clan from the guardianship of the Palace gates, and substituting the clans of Satsuma, Tosa and Geishiu. On the same day the In no Miya and Nijô were dismissed, and the offices of Kuambaku and Shôgun were abolished. Three kinds of offices, called Sôsai, Gijô and Sanyo, were provisionally instituted, and various Court nobles (*kugé*), territorial princes (*daimiô*), and *samurai* were appointed to fill them, and to carry on the administration. A decree was also issued announcing that the Government of the country was henceforth solely in the hands of the Imperial Court.

Some time before this, whilst Tokugawa Naifu still held the office of Shôgun, he, Shimadzu and three other princes had memorialized the Court with a view to the recall of the seven court nobles (who in 1863 fled to Chôshiu), and the summoning of the house of Môri to the capital. These propositions being approved, the Bakufu sent for a member of the Môri family to communicate the order, whereupon Môri Takumi arrived at Hiôgo in Setsu, as the representative of the prince, at the head of eight hundred men, whom the Bakufu was desirous of locating at Ôzaka. The commander, Yamada Ichinojô, and his lieutenant Kôno Jiurô refused, and prepared to enter the capital without passing through Ôzaka. As soon, however, as the Government came into the hands of the Imperial Court, it at once summoned the Chôshiu clan to Kiôto. The troops started immediately from Hiôgo and arrived at Kiôto on the 5th of January. A decree was immediately issued by which all their honours and titles were restored to the members of the House of Môri, and shortly afterwards the seven court nobles also re-entered the capital.

Although peace had been made between Tokugawa and Môri, it seemed as if the feeling of mutual hostility engendered by the war had not completely died out, and the Aidzu *samurai*, in particular, were dissatisfied. They were extremely unwilling to be considered on a level with the Chôshiu men, and were highly offended at their presence in the capital. Tokugawa Naifu himself was also bitterly mortified by the order to turn out his troops from the Palace which had been issued on the 3rd, and his views undergoing a complete change, he at last summoned the Aidzu clan and others of his adherents to a council at the castle of Nijô. He then addressed them as follows: "Why has the policy of the Court altered thus in the last "few days? There must be some one who, in order to "succeed in a plot, is misleading the young Emperor." Annoyed at having been excluded from participation in the measures adopted on the 3rd, he informed the Court that he would act upon its previous order, and take charge of affairs; that order having declared that everything should be determined by a council of princes to be assembled at the capital. The conduct of the Naifu in sending up such a memorial after having surrendered the governing power caused him to be regarded with general distrust.

The Palace at this moment was guarded by Satsuma, Chôshiu, Tosa, Geishiu and various other princes, while the greater part of the Tokugawa family's troops occupied the castle of Nijô, and seemed to be keeping a keen watch on the movements of the others. The public feeling was very uneasy, and various rumours flew about. Some of the Tokugawa officers and men advised the Naifu not to submit tamely to the will of his opponents, but to occupy Ôzaka in force, and so block up their line of communications, which would enable him to control their actions.

The Naifu consented, and leaving a letter behind for the Court, in which he pretended that he was going away to Ôzaka in order to calm the passions of his retainers, suddenly proceeded thither on the night of the 6th at the head of the troops, accompanied by the princes of Aidzu and Kuwana and Itakura Iga no kami (his chief adviser). The court considered this proceeding so suspicious that it prohibited the clans of Kuwana and Aidzu from re-entering the capital.

As soon as the news was brought to Yedo measures were actively taken for putting the city in a condition of defence. For some time previously the troops of Sakai Sayémon no Jô had patrolled the streets. It happened also that several hundred *rônins* had concealed themselves in the Satsuma *yashiki* situated in that quarter of the city called Shiba, and having formed themselves into a corps, were in the habit of sallying forth by night to plunder the richer citizens. On one occasion they also fired into the Sakai barracks, and a great commotion ensued. The Sakai troops, inflamed with anger, begged for leave to attack the Satsuma *yashiki*, and the matter being referred to Ôzaka, it seemed to Tokugawa Naifu that the recent change in the councils of the Mikado was due to the influence of the Satsuma *samurai*, and that the same clan had no doubt been hounding on the *rônins* to disturb the peace of the Kuantô. He therefore sent orders to Yedo for the chastisement of the rioters. The Tokugawa officials proceeded to surround the Satsuma *yashiki*, burnt it, and made the whole band prisoners. From this moment the Tokugawa and Shimadzu were bitter enemies, and the Naifu sent up a memorial in which he complained of the robberies committed by the Satsuma clan in the Kuantô, and prayed the Mikado to dismiss all the *samurai* of that clan who had any share in the government. The Court, however, took no notice of his representations.

The Gijô and Sanyo then took counsel together, saying: "Although the Imperial family is now in possession of "the Goverment, it has no means of meeting its ex-"penses. The Tokugawa and other clans should be made "to contribute." The Mikado therefore ordered Owari Dainagon and Matsudaira Shungaku to go and talk over the Naifu, who was to be made a Gijô. They were accompanied by Narusé Hayato no kami, Tanaka Fujimaro, Washidzu Kidô and Menjiu Hiroshi, and proceeding to Ôzaka communicated the wishes of the Court, offering at the same time to admit the Naifu to the Mikado's presence. They also advised him under present circumstances to dismiss all feelings of resentment, and to bring but a small escort with him to Kiôto. If he felt uneasy about his safety, they, his relations, would guard him with their troops. The Naifu expressed his innocence of any treasonable intentions, and promised to obey the Mikado's orders, but in his heart he disliked the proposal. When he first went down to Ôzaka, he had left Kondô Isami, leader of the corps called Shinsen-gumi, Hijikata Saizô, commander of the infantry, and others, at Fushimi, and at this moment the number of the eastern troops stationed in that town amounted to several thousands. Washidzu and his colleagues therefore remarked to Nagai Gemba no kami and Tsukahara Tajima no kami, who were in chief command, that as the Naifu, in obedience to the Mikado's orders, was about to appear at Court, it was absolutely necessary that the troops should be withdrawn from Fushimi, and they enlarged repeatedly on the duty of submission. Nagai and his colleague were willing to comply, but they had not power to carry out their promise. On the 25th of January the two ex-princes of Owari and Echizen returned to Kiôto and reported that Tokugawa Naifu had promised obedience to the Imperial orders, but they did this in ignorance of his real intentions.

The same night the princes of Aidzu and Kuwana and their chief retainers assembled at Ôzaka, and addressed the Naifu as follows: "No faith can be placed in the declara-"tions of the ex-princes of Owari and Echizen. If your "Highness determines to go, your servants will follow "even at the risk of their own lives. On this expedition "we will remove from the Emperor his bad counsellors, "and try the issue with them by the sword." Hereupon the Naifu made up his mind, and determined to enter Kiôto with the clans of Aidzu and Kuwana in the front of his following.

When this news reached the capital the public feeling was much excited. The Court sent the clans of Satsuma and Chôshiu to lie outside the capital, and blocking up the Fushimi and Toba roads, to obstruct the advance of the eastern army. The leaders Ijichi Shôji (of Satsuma) and Yamada Ichinojô (of Chôshiu) accepted the duty, saying: "Your servants have ascertained by means of spies "that strange things are on foot at Ôzaka, and they "believe that a large force will endeavour to force its "way past the barriers. We pray, therefore, for leave to "act as the emergency may require." The Court gave them orders to the effect that, although Tokugawa Naifu was permitted to enter the capital, he could not be allowed to do so at the head of a large force. As for the clans of Aidzu and Kuwana, admission was to be absolutely denied to them, and instructions were given to them to act according to circumstances. The commanders then bade their men to make preparations for resistance, and quietly to await the course of events. The Kiôto forces at this moment numbered some six thousand five hundred men, while the eastern army was reported to be thirty thousand strong. Sakuma Ômi no kami and Kubota Bizen no kami* headed the drilled troops on the Tokugawa side, while the troops of Takamatsu, Hamada, and other princes

---

* Formerly commander of the Japanese garrison at Yokohama.

subject to the ex-Shôgun acted as a reserve. The clans of Aidzu and Kuwana marched in the van, and were ready to advance by the Fushimi and Toba roads.

On the 27th the messengers of the House of Tokugawa came to the barriers which had been placed on both roads and asked leave to pass, which was refused by the sentries. The messengers then said: "Our prince is going to Court "by the order of the Mikado, and if you venture to ob- "struct his passage he will force his way through." Having said this they departed, and then the great force began to approach. The Kiôto forces, seeing that matters had come to a head, discharged their artillery, to which the easterners replied with a volley from their muskets. The ordnance thundered for a while, but the Kiôto forces eventually put the enemy to flight. At this moment a fire broke out in the town of Fushimi, and the easterners came again by both roads to attack the Kiôto forces, who defended themselves vigorously. After having lost several killed and wounded both combatants retired from the field about six in the evening. At midnight spies were sent from the Kiôto side to see what the enemy who had advanced by the Toba road might be doing, and they returned with information that he was quartered there and was taking food. Orders were given to surprise him, and the easterners, entirely losing their presence of mind, flung down their weapons and fled. The reserves, however, coming up to their aid, the defeated troops plucked up courage, and rallied again to the fight. They charged fiercely into the Kiôto forces, and threw them into disorder, but the captains Ichiki, Ôyama and Gotô, encouraging their men, met the attack and fell upon the left wing of the eastern army, which began to waver. The Kiôto forces profited by this and engaged them vigorously, so that the eastern army was at last defeated, but the three captains above-mentioned were killed. The Kiôto forces withdrew at two p.m. (for two a.m. ?) from the field of battle.

190   At eight o'clock on the morning of the 28th the two armies fought again on the Fushimi and Toba roads. The Kiôto party had placed some skirmishers in a bamboo thicket at the side of the Toba road. When the eastern army pressed up along the two roads in great force, the Kiôto troops opposed them with energy, Yamada Magoichirô and Ijiu-in Kinjirô distinguishing themselves by their courage. At last the enemy was put to flight on the Fushimi road, while from Toba he advanced with greater determination than ever, and his ferocity was terrible. Some of the rebels' bullets actually struck the gold brocade standard of the Mikado, which the commander-in-chief, Prince Ninnaji, had ordered to be carried before him as he advanced. At this moment the men in ambush fired a simultaneous volley from the thicket, and the bullets fell in the centre of the rebels as thick as hailstones, laying low immense numbers of them. The loyal forces [50] on the road profited by this opportunity to charge the rebel van, which scattered in all directions, the fugitives tramping on the dead and dying in their hurry to escape. Immediately afterwards fires broken out in the village of Toba, and the rebels retreated to the town of Yodo. In this engagement Sakuma Ômi, Kubota Bizen and many other rebel officers were killed, while the loyal forces lost Kajiki, Hiraoka and some twenty or thirty more.

191   At dawn on the 29th the loyal army attacked Yodo, which the rebels defended from the other end of the bridge. The loyal forces then directed a steady artillery fire against the town, to which the rebels replied. Neither party seeming willing to advance, the rebels lodged a corps of one hundred spearmen in the rushes by the side of the river, and a party of musketeers was sent out to provoke an attack from the loyal army, but the latter, knowing of the embuscade, did not move. But a Captain

---

(50) The common Japanese expression is *Kuan-gun*, of which 'Government army' would be the most literal rendering, but 'loyal army,' is a more convenient equivalent for ordinary use.

named Ishikawa Wakasa no suké said: "We shall be "laughed at if we lose a good chance because we see dan- "ger," and with these words, he attacked the rebels at the head of a small number of musketeers. The rest were excited by the example, and shouting out: " We must not " sacrifice our troops to the enemy for nothing," followed the others eagerly. Upon this this the men in ambush arose to right and left of them, and the musketeers came on again in large numbers. Ishikawa, Itô and Nakajima were killed, but Yamada, Ijiu-In, Fujimura, Miura and other captains, rousing their men to the same height of enthusiasm as they were themselves animated by, charged the foe, whose ranks began to fall into disorder. Their men then raised a shout and finally succeeded in routing the rebels. They took the castle of Yodo about noon, while the rebels retiring in a body held Hashimoto.

192. The Tsu clan (from Isé) had been holding the barrier at Yamazaki in the interests of the eastern army, but an envoy was sent to them by the Mikado, who enlarged upon the duty of obedience and talked them over. In obedience to the Mikado's orders they admitted the loyal forces, but the rebels at Hashimoto (on the opposite bank of the river) knew nothing of their defection.

193 On the 30th the loyal forces prepared to attack Hashi- moto. On the preceding day the rebels had wished to occupy the castle of Yodo, but the *samurai* of that clan refused to admit them, and they were forced therefore to find lodgings in the town. When the loyal forces arrived at the castle, they suspected the clan of siding with the enemy, and reproached them, upon which they related how they had repelled the rebels, in order to prove their sincerity. The Yodo troops were then placed in the van, and an attack was made on Hashimoto, which the rebel army stoutly defended, until a flank fire of artillery was opened upon their head quarters from the redoubt at Yamazaki, by which a large number of them were killed.

The whole army broke and fled, pursued by the loyal forces, down to Ôzaka. Before this, news of the daily defeats had been received there, and Tokugawa Naifu, the princes of Aidzu and Kuwana, Itakura Iga, Ogasawara Iki and the rest of the officials had betaken themselves in a hurry on board of a man-of-war, in which they fled eastwards. The castle of Ôzaka was burnt immediately afterward.

144 On the 2nd of February Prince Ninnaji no Miya advanced and entered Ôzaka. In this short campaign the Satsuma clan had one hundred and fifty men killed, including Ijiu-In Yoichi, while the Chôshiu clan lost Katayama Kinjirô and one hundred and twenty more. These large losses arose from the fact of these two clans alone having been opposed to an enemy far superior in numbers, but their reputation for valour rose immensely.

145 The loyal forces having thus achieved a great victory sent detachments against Takamatsu and other clans, in order to bring the whole of the neighbouring provinces into order, and to enforce obedience. All the clans changed their policy and submitted.

146 When the eastern forces first occupied the castle of Nijô the Court Nobles had been in dire state of fright, dreading lest hostilities should be commenced in the capital itself, but they were considerably relieved when the ex-Shôgun made his retreat to Ôzaka. The commanders Ijichi Shôji and Yamada Ichinojô, and the lieutenant Kôno Jiurô, were dissatisfied, and said to themselves: "Since ancient "times nearly all attacks on Kiôto have been successful. "The Eastern army has retreated for no good purpose. "They intend to occupy Ôzaka, cut off our means of ob- "taining supplies, bring the troops of Kuantô up by the "Tôkaidô, and then by blockading Hiôgo with their fleet, "to catch us like rats in a cage." So they resolved upon sending troops to the provinces of Tajima, Tamba and Tango, to seize that tract of country, and to retreat thither

for a while, if the necessity arose, and there lay their plans for a second attempt. Hardly had they arrived at this determination when the war broke out, and they at once despatched thither a body of three hundred picked men under the command of a court noble named Saionji Chiunagon, but victory declaring itself on the side of the Mikado the necessity for a retreat did not arise. At the same time the presence of Saionji in those parts had a good effect in determining the local *daimiôs* to submit. The ✓ public praised the completeness of the Imperial tactics.

197 Three thousand Kishiu troops had been encamped at the temple of Tennôji, close to Ôzaka, and when the war broke out their leaders secretly despatched a messenger to the loyal army to ask for instructions. The councillors at-war deliberated, saying: "Although the loyalty of the Ki-"shiu clan is well-known, the prince is a relative of the "ex-Shôgun, and we cannot be sure of his intentions. The "best plan would be to send them away from Ôzaka back "to their native province." This decision being reported by the messenger, the Kishiu troops returned home. Hikoné, Ôgaki and other clans had already joined the royal army, and by this time all the princes of the centre and ✓ west of Japan supported the Mikado.

198 It is said that when the proposal was made to return to the ancient form of Government by the sovereign, Saigô Kichinoské, who was behind the scenes, disapproved of the use of force, and that the war was caused by the change which the policy of the Tokugawa family went at a critical moment. The public remarked freely upon the fact that the Naifu had acted contrary to his own convic- ✓ tions.

199 On the 5th of February the Court deprived Tokugawa Naifu and his followers of all their honours and dignities, and published a proclamation throughout the country, saying, "After Tokugawa Keiki retired to Ôzaka upon a "certain pretence, the ex-princes of Owari and Echizen

" were sent thither to summon him to Kiôto, in order to
" come to an arrangement. Keiki had already been for-
" bidden to enter Kiôto with a large train. He declared,
" however, that he would come to Court, with the clans of
" Aidzu and Kuwana at the head of his following, and
" actually approached the capital. This was not obedience
" to the Mikado, and was, in fact, an attack upon His
" Majesty. The loyal forces resisted his advance in the
" environs of the capital, and hostilities broke out. Keiki
" still continued to place his vassals in the field, and for
" several days in succession fired upon the imperial stand-
" ard. Having been defeated he has fled to the east, but
" he cannot escape the consequences of his criminal at-
" tempt to deceive the Imperial Court. It has therefore
" been resolved to send a large army to subdue his ter-
" ritories." All the clans were called upon to furnish
troops and Prince Arisugawa was appointed Commander-
in-Chief of the Army of Chastisement, a brocade banner
and a sword of justice being granted to him.

At this moment all the foreign representatives were at
Kôbé, whence they issued a declaration of neutrality on
the 18th of February, and proclaimed to their countrymen
resident there, saying : " A civil war is about to break out
" between the eastern and western portions of Japan. The
" people of our nations must not help either party, nor sell
" arms to them." This was because the Tokugawa affair
was not yet settled.

END OF VOL. II.

VOLUME III.

The governing power having now reverted to the Imperial Court, it took steps to inform the foreign representatives of the fact that Kiôto would henceforth be the seat of the Japanese Government. This announcement was received with due submission, and the representatives then said: "During the last few years some forty or fifty of "our countrymen have been killed by yours, and inex- "pressible grief has been caused by these acts. As the "sovereign has now freshly assumed the ruling power, "let him give an order throughout the country prohibiting "such deeds." The court thereupon issued a general proclamation.

But there were still many in the country who hated foreigners, and on the 8th of March, some Tosa men fired on sixteen French sailors at Sakai in Idzumi, killing some and wounding others. Already a Bizen man had assassinated a Frenchman at Kôbé in Setsu,[51] and this together with the more recent affair excited the anger of the French Minister, who accordingly made five demands on the Government. Firstly, that a high officer of the Government should go on board the French man-of-war to make an

(51) This affair occurred on the 4th February. The Frenchman said to have been 'assassinated' only received a slight wound, and an American seaman was shot through the body. As the attack was directed generally upon all the foreigners who happened to be in the street at the time the Foreign Representatives demanded that capital punishment should be inflicted on the officer who had given the order to fire.

apology. Secondly, that no Japanese officer should be allowed to enter the foreign settlements with swords on.[52] Thirdly, that an indemnity of one hundred and fifty thousand dollars should be paid. Fourthly, that the Government should make a written apology. Fifthly, that the Japanese soldiers who were implicated in this murderous act should be capitally punished. He also insisted on the acceptance of these demands within three days, threatening that if this limit were exceeded he would resort to other measures. The Government was at this moment deeply engaged in reorganizing the administration, and feeling also that the wrong was on the side of Japan, at once accepted four[53] of the five articles. Sixteen Tosa and Bizen men were arrested and decapitated on the 18th March.[54] Thus the matter was settled.

The ex-Prince of Uwajima and Higashi-Kuzé Shôshô had already informed the foreign Representatives at Ôzaka that a Department of Foreign Affairs having been formed with themselves placed at its head, they desired henceforth to act in concert. Also, that the Mikado wished to see the Representatives at Kiôto before long. The Representatives replied that they had been informed that an expedition was about to be sent against the House of Tokugawa, and that they proposed to return at once to Yokohama to provide for the safety of their countrymen. If the Mikado wished to see them the matter could be arranged at once. They requested, therefore, that a day might be fixed. Higashi-kuzé answered that he and his colleague would be responsible for the safety of the foreigners at Yokohama and Hakodaté. The Representa-

---

(52) The second demand was that Tosa troops should not enter any of the open ports.

(53) Was the second demand not insisted on? The Parliamentary Papers do not mention its having been withdrawn.

(54) The Bizen officer was executed on the evening of March 3rd; eighteen Tosa soldiers and two officers were likewise condemned to suffer death, and the sentence was duly carried out in the case of eleven of their number, the other nine being reprieved at the request of the French Authorities. This was on the 16th March.

tives need be under no apprehensions on that score. The Representatives responded that nevertheless they could not wait long. Upon this the Court, after debating, fixed a day. Some persons remarked that to invite the barbarians to the Palace would cause public comment, but one of the Sanyo laughed and treated the idea with contempt. On the 23rd as the English Representative was going to Court some *rônins* suddenly made an attack on him, and wounded some of his escort. The Japanese officials and the English guards repelled the attack, and killed the *rônins*, so that nothing serious resulted. The Representative, however, returned home without going through the ceremony.

During the same month, in order that the nature of its intended policy might be understood, the Court proclaimed throughout the country that foreign relations would be continued. This was in accordance with the precedent contained in the Imperial sanction given to the Treaties in the preceding reign.

On the 24th [55] the English Representative had an interview with the Tennô, and the Dutch, American and French Representatives were presented after him. They congratulated His Majesty on the magnificence of the Imperial rule, and gave renewed promise of friendly relations. It is said that when the Kôbé and Sakai affairs occurred the functionaries were much troubled in their minds, lamenting the uncertain future of the Empire. But now foreign affairs had been settled, the home provinces were quiet, and the *samurai* and lower classes of the capital gave themselves up to rejoicing.

About this time the Councillor of State Ôkubo addressed a memorial to the Mikado, saying : "Although Your "Majesty's forces have been victorious in the battles of

---

(55) The English Minister had his audience of the Mikado on the 20th March, the French and Dutch Ministers having been presented on the 23rd. The American Minister did not visit Kiôto with his colleagues, and was therefore not presented on his occasion.

" Fushimi and Toba the ringleader of the rebels has made
" his escape. The dispositions of the various clans are
" uncertain, and our relations with foreign countries are
" not on a satisfactory footing. Extreme measures are
" necessary in a crisis. Since the middle ages our Em-
" peror has lived behind a screen, and has never trodden
" the earth. Nothing of what went on outside his screen
" ever penetrated to his sacred ear; the imperial resi-
" dence was profoundly secluded, and naturally unlike the
" outer world. No more than a few court nobles were
" allowed to approach the throne, a practice most opposed
" to the principles of Heaven. Although it is the first duty
" of man to respect his superior, if he reveres that su-
" perior too highly he neglects his duty, while a breach is
" created between the sovereign and his subjects, who are
" unable to convey their wants to him. This vicious
" practice has been common in all ages. But now let
" pompous etiquette be done away with, and simplicity
" become our first object. Kiôto is in an out-of-the-way
" position, and is unfit to be the seat of government. Let
" His Majesty take up his abode temporarily at Ôzaka,
" removing his capital thither, and thus cure one of the
" hundred abuses which we inherit from past ages. This
" seems to me to be a matter of great urgency, and I
" humbly pray your wisdom to decide this without loss of
" time." This memorial produced a lively effect on the
Court, and to the advice contained in it the subsequent
removal of the Mikado to Yedo was no doubt due.

During the same month the public notice boards
throughout the country were taken down and replaced by
new ones.

The castle of Nijô had been converted into an office for
the Council of State (*Da-jô-kan*), where its members met
to decide upon what measures should be adopted. The
Mikado proceeded thither in person and, in the presence
of the assembled Court nobles and the territorial princes,

took an oath. By this oath he promised that a deliberative assembly should be formed, and all measures be decided by public opinion; that the uncivilised customs of former ✓ times should be broken through, and the impartiality and justice displayed in the workings of nature be adopted as a basis of action; and that intellect and learning should be sought for throughout the world, in order to establish the foundations of the empire. A discussion then ensued as to the best means of developing the resources of Yezo. Shortly afterwards the Mikado went down to Ôzaka as the first stage in his personal campaign against the adherents of the fallen power, and inspected the fleet.

During this time the loyal army was marching to the attack of Yedo by various roads. The troops of Satsuma, Kishiu, Chôshiu, Tôdô, Bizen, Sadowara, Kuméyama, Minakuchi, Ômura, Inshiu, Higo and Echizen advanced along the Tôkaidô. Another detachment of Satsuma troops, with those of Inshiu, Tosa, and Ôgaki advanced by the Nakasendô.

Reports of the approach of the loyal forces reached Yedo day after day. The retainers of the Tokugawa family and the *samurai* of the subject clans *(fudai)* met together in council of war. During the war at Fushimi and Toba a party had arisen in the two clans of Kishiu and Owari which advocated supporting the ex-Shôgun, as head of the Tokugawa family, and placed itself in communication with Yedo. The ex-Prince of Owari, who was annoyed at this, having taken counsel with his retainers Kosé Shintarô, Tamiya Joun, Tanaka Fujimaro, Washidzu Kidô and Niwa Juntarô, issued a proclamation that loyalty must take precedence of affection for relatives. He inflicted death upon Watanabé Shinzaëmon, Sakakibara Kagéyu, Ishikawa Kuranojô, Teraö Takéshirô, Tsukada Kakushirô and eight other ringleaders, besides confiscating the revenues of Suzuki Tango, Narusé Buzen, and fifteen more; some of whom he threw into prison, others being confined to their own houses. In this way the views of the whole clan were rendered uniformly loyal to the Mikado. On the other hand, those of the Kishiu clan who happened to be at Yedo bent all their efforts towards aiding the chief of the family, and took part in the plans of the Tokugawa retainers. Kondô Isami and his friends also happened to be there, and consultations were held day and night at the castle. Some proposed to send a force to occupy the pass of Hakoné, while others suggested a naval attack upon Ôzaka. These plans they pressed upon the attention of Keiki, and completely robbed him of his rest and appetite. But the ex-Shôgun already repented of his late conduct, and animated by a spirit of respectful obedience, refused to entertain their proposals. He summoned Katsu Awa and Ôkubo Ichiô to a private chamber, and then addressed a letter to his retainers, prohibiting them from resisting the imperial forces, and added that those who did so would be pointing their weapons against himself. Immediately afterwards he quitted the castle, and retired into voluntary confinement in the monastery of Kuanyeiji at Uyéno.

Keiki's fanatical retainers were excessively disgusted with his submissiveness, and they all began to collect troops with the intention of acting independently of him. Some of them fled into Hitachi and Kôdzuké together with the Drilled Troops, and some into the province of Kai. The Tosa and Inshiu forces, having advanced from Shinano into Kai, had taken the town of Kôfu, and the Tokugawa vassals there, entering into a plot with those who had run away from Yedo, erected a stockade at the town of Katsunama, and occupied the hills, harassing the loyal troops. The Tosa troops forced the stockade, and surprised the enemy's rear, on which the rebels destroyed all the bridges along the road, and constructing batteries out of gabions, resisted their advance. Upon the loyal forces attacking them with firearms, they set fire to the houses of the common people, so as to prevent an advance. Unable to overcome this obstacle, detachments of Tosa and Inshiu troops climbed the hills on both sides, attacked the rebels and succeeded in routing them, killing or capturing nearly all. Leaving the town of Kôfu in charge of the house of Sanada (Matsushiro) the Inshiu and Tosa forces pursued their march towards Yedo.

During the course of this month the Satsuma, Chôshiu and Ôgaki troops arrived at Haniu in Musashi, and engaging the runaway troops assembled at Yamada, inflicted a severe defeat on them. They then advanced, and laid siege to the town of Oshi-no-Giôda. When the runaways first visited that town the clansmen had secretly given aid to them, and upon the approach of the Imperial forces, one of the commanders disembowelled himself by way of expiation, and the rest of the clan joined the Mikado's banner. Upon this the young noble Iwakura, who commanded the Nakasendô column, took up his quarters at the town of Itabashi (just outside Yedo).

By this time the Prince Commander-in-Chief had arrived at the town of Sumpu on the Tôkaidô at the head of his forces, while Keiki, worn out by trouble and anxiety, was respectfully awaiting his commands in a small room at Uyéno. Rinnôji no Miya and the *Shittô*[56] Gakuô-In, moved by pity for him, proceeded to Sumpu and begged for mercy, while Kazu Miya and Tenshô-In[57] also sent some of their women as messengers along the Tôkaidô. These envoys followed each other in rapid succession. Shortly follow the vanguard advanced to Shinagawa, whither at once came Katsu Awa to see Saigô Kichinoské,[58] the military adviser of the royal army. Having fully explained the

---
(56) *Shittô* was an office corresponding to the *Soba-yônin*, or man of business, of a *daimiô*.
(57) Widows of the Shôgun Iyémochi and Iyésada.
(58) Takamori is the name by which he is mentioned in the original, but he is best known to both Japanese and foreigners by his common appellation (*zokumiô*) of Kichinoské.

submissive temper of Keiki, he begged that the loyal army would desist from making an attack. Katsu was an old acquaintance of Saigô's and repeated his visits frequently, using all the eloquence at his command in support of his prayers. Saigô at last replied that he would leave the matter to the decision of the Miya Commanding-in-Chief, and demanded material guarantees of good faith. Katsu promised to give these, and Saigô addressed a letter to the Miya Commanding-in-Chief, who after consulting with those about him, issued the necessary orders to the various divisions of the army. In this way Yedo was preserved from an assault, and was occupied by the loyal army, which took up its quarters in different parts of the town.

On the 26th of April the Mikado's envoy made his entry into the castle of Yedo. The retainers of the Tokugawa family swept the roads clean and went forth to meet him in their best clothes. At the interview which took place between the envoy and Tayasu Chiunagon the former announced the Mikado's will, as follows: " Deliver up the castle, the men-of-war, and all your fire-arms. Condemn to a punishment one degree less severe than death those who aided Keiki in his rebellion, and report thereon. Keiki's life will be spared, and he must confine himself at the town of Mito." The Chiunagon signified his readiness to obey, but when the seditiously inclined members of the clan heard of the terms granted they absconded to the north-east in large bodies. After the lapse of three days Keiki retired to Mito.

Aidzu Katamori had previously retired to his territory, while Itakura Iga, Ogasawara Iki and their friends had concealed themselves in the north-east. Some of the hereditary subject *daimiôs* of the Tokugawa family who were at Yedo went up to Kiôto, while others retreated to their territories. The result was that the city became quite deserted.

The *samurai* of Aidzu and the runaway troops had been engaged for some time in talking over the *daimiôs* and rich inhabitants of Kadzusa, Shimôsa Shimotsuké and Kôdzuké, and had collected both money and provisions. They were joined by Midzuno Hiuga, the prince of Yûki, but Obata Heima and some others of his retainers, amounting to sixty men in all, adopted loyal views, and placing the prince's son at their head, expelled Hiuga and the runaway troops. Shortly afterwards Hiuga and the runaway troops attacked and took the castle, after having killed Obata and his party. The son fled and sought refuge with the loyal army, and the rebels began to show a formidable front. At this moment the troops of Hikoné and other clans were in occupation of Utsunomiya, which the rebels, presuming upon their strength, formed the design of taking. On the alarm being brought to Itabashi the Military adviser Kagawa Keijô, with Arima of the Satsuma clan, Soshiki of the Chôshiu clan, Uyéda of the Tosa clan and others, advanced to Senji at the head of three hundred men. A detachment of rebels had occupied Nagaréyama, but upon being suddenly attacked by the loyal forces, found themselves unable to make a stand, and throwing away their weapons, took to flight. The loyal forces followed in pursuit and captured their leader Kondô Isami, who was sent to Itabashi in a cage. This man had long been celebrated for his intrepid courage. In the winter of 1868, when the Shôgun retired to Ôzaka, he had commanded the van as far as Fushimi, where he finally remained to obstruct the passage of the loyal troops. When the war broke out he directed the movements of the troops, receiving a bullet-wound in the thigh, and upon the defeat of the Eastern army, accompanied it in its flight to Yedo. Having incited some of the Tokugawa retainers to proceed with him to Kôshiu, he effected a junction with the local troops, and offered resistance to the Tosa and Inshiu forces at the town of Katsunuma, but being defeated, fled with the men under his command to the vicinity of Yedo. The loyal forces, having at last captured him, put him to death, and sent his head preserved in *saké* to Kiôto, where it was pilloried on the dry bed of the river close to Shijô. This was done because during the last few years he had to a great extent assisted in the counsels of the Aidzu clan at Kiôto.

The rebel troops at Nagaréyama having now been annihilated, Kagawa and Soshiki profited by their victory to advance into Shimotsuké and attack the castle of Yûki. Hiuga and the rebel troops with him abandoned the place and fled. Soshiki at once occupied the castle at the head of the troops of the Susaka clan, while Kagawa and the other commanders proceeded to Utsunomiya with the Hikoné troops. Shortly afterwards the rebel leader Ôtori Keiské came to attack Yûki at the head of all his men, and having re-taken it, he made it the basis of his further operations. The loyal forces fled to Utsunomiya.

On the 9th of May Ôtori Keiské advanced to the town of Oyama at the head of two thousand men, and attacked the loyal army. The troops of Hikoné, Akimoto, Ôgaki and Kasama went out to meet him, but owing to the use made by the enemy of skirmishers, were unable to hold their ground. A Chôshiu captain named Nambu and an Akimoto captain named Ishikawa, besides others, lost their lives. At four o'clock in the afternoon the loyal army retreated to Utsunomiya, while the rebels took up their quarters at the town of Tochigi. In this engagement the Hikoné troops suffered the greatest loss in killed and wounded.

On the 11th, before day-break, Ôtori Keiské made another attack on Utsunomiya at the head of his whole force. He was resisted by the troops of Matsumoto, Kurohané, Kasama, Mibu, Toki, Iwamurata, Susaka, Hikoné, Ôgaki and Utsunomiya, who met him outside the castle, but the rebels fought with such desperation that the loyal forces were compelled to retreat and occupy the castle. At the same time another detachment of rebels advanced on their flank from Kanuma, while the Aidzu clan also advanced by the Sannô Pass,[59] and an united attack was now made on the castle. The noise of artillery resounded on all sides, until the loyal forces, becoming at last unable to continue the defence, abandoned the castle and dispersed. The *daimiô* fled to Tatébayashi. Itakura Iga was in the castle, having some time previously surrendered to the Hikoné forces, and he fell into the hands of the rebels, in whose complete possession the town of Utsunomiya now was.

The rebel leader, Ôtori Keiské, was an excellent strategist and manœuvred his men with the greatest ease. Most of the troops at his disposal had been drilled by Frenchmen, so that their good discipline and valour caused much trouble to the loyal forces. The latter were accustomed to look upon him as equivalent to a whole nation of enemies.

Although the clans of the neighbourhood had all joined the loyal forces after the battles of Oyama and Takei, their men were usually defeated by the enemy owing to their wearing armour and using only swords and spears. The rebels were therefore enabled to occupy all the most important positions one after the other. An appeal for aid was therefore made to Itabashi and Yedo. The Imperial Court prepared to despatch reinforcements, and the order to march was given to the troops of Satsuma, Chôshiu, Ôgaki, Tosa and Inshiu. They started forthwith, and, having effected a junction with the troops of the local clans at Mibu, attacked Utsunomiya in force on the morning of the 14th. The rebel forces issued forth from the castle to a distance of about one *ri* to resist the royal army, which advanced to engage them at

---

(59) On the boundary of Mutsu and Shimotsuké, near a place called Ikari, between Wakamatsu and Utsunomiya.

Yasudzuka. Upon this the rebels suddenly fell upon the rear of the vanguard, composed of Satsuma and Ôgaki troops, by a bye-road, and the bullets fell like hail, so that the loyal forces were almost routed. But a detachment of their fellow clansmen coming up to their aid from the town of Suzumé-no-miya, they were enabled to rally, and finally put the rebels to flight. The latter then occupied the castle and the temples of Miôjin and Hachiman, whence they discharged their cannon, and the loyal forces surrounding them on all sides responded to their fire. The discharges from both sides shook the whole country round, and the smoke rose up to heaven in such volumes that no man could distinguish his neighbour's face. At six o'clock in the evening the rebels still maintained their position and kept up a cannonade against the loyal troops, many of whom were killed and wounded. Kawada Sakuma, an Inshiu captain, became enraged, and said: "I am profoundly indignant "that so many of our soldiers should be lost for the sake "of a herd of rebels. We will exterminate them before "the sun sets and take the castle. Here, all of you exert "yourselves." So saying, he shouted loud, and endeavoured to inspire the rest with the enthusiasm he felt. The Inshiu troops were excited to desperation, and climbing up into the castle, captured one of its faces. At this moment the general attack became fiercer, and the rebels giving way, the castle and both temples were deserted simultaneously by their occupants, who broke through the attacking line, and fled to Nikkô. By the time the loyal forces recovered the castle, the sun had set. It is said that the rebles were enabled to make such a determined stand because deserters from neighbouring clans had joined them, and the loyal forces were sore fatigued after the assault.

Even after this Ôtori Keiské made frequent sallies from the vicinity of Nikkô. The Tosa troops encountered him at Imaichi without any decisive result. Shortly afterwards the loyal forces inflicted a severe defeat on the rebels, most of whom dispersed, and Ôtori was compelled to take refuge in Aidzu with the few men who still remained to him.

Some time earlier a number of runaway vassals of the Tokugawa family had taken up a position at Kisaradzu in Kadzusa, where they collected large quantities of provisions. The Miya Commanding-in-chief despatched troops to attack them, upon which they advanced to the town of Funahashi. At this moment the Bizen troops happened to be at Yawata; those of Tôdô were at Kaidzuka; the Chikuzen men at Giôtoku, and the Sadowara troops at Kamagaya. Before dawn on the 15th of June the rebels suddenly sallied forth and attacked the quarters occupied by Tôdô and Bizen, to the great discomfiture of those clans. The rebels profited by the advantage thus gained to pour in a heavy fire, the two clans retreating as they fought. In this way the pursuit continued as far as the ferry at Ichikawa, where many of the clansmen were drowned in their hurry to reach the boats. As soon as the Sadowara troops heard the sound of artillery they started from Kamagaya, but were intercepted on their march by another rebel detachment. They concealed themselves in a field of millet, and throwing out skirmishers, fired with steady aim at the rebels, many of whom fell. They then opened fire with a mortar and put the remainder to flight. At this moment the main body of the rebels had defeated the loyal forces at Yawata and Kaidzuka, and having quartered themselves at Funahashi, were taking their food. The Sadowara troops, after having ascertained this by means of spies, separated into three bodies; one of which advanced along the seashore to the rear of Funahashi, while a second took the main road and the third proceeded along a byepath. In this way they suddenly surprised the place, and the rebels defended themselves in wild confusion. Fortunately the Chikuzen, Tôdô and Bizen troops came charging up, and they all attacked the rebels in conjunction. As the latter fought in the most desperate manner, the loyal forces set fire to the town, and burnt their den. The smoke and flames filled the sky, and the rebels falling finally into confusion, fled in all directions. Three days after this all the runaway troops in Kadzusa had been annihilated.

During this month Sanjô Sadaishô was residing at Yedo in the quality of *Kansasshi*[60]. The Imperial Court made Tayasu Kaménoské successor to the headship of the Tokugawa family, and the decree of investment was conveyed to him by the *Kansasshi*. The reason of this proceeding was that the ex-Shôgun had already given satisfactory proofs of repentance. The value of the fief was however not yet determined, and his retainers murmured loudly. When Katsu Awa became so frequent a visitor to the loyal army, as before narrated, those who entertained violent opinions had been offended with his proceedings, and had secretly plotted to assassinate him; and when the castle, together with all the munitions of war, had afterwards to be given up, they were more displeased than ever. Hereupon they assumed the name of *Shôgitai* (lity. the Band which makes duty clear) and seized Tôyeizan[61]. The chief members of the Tokugawa family had for generations been buried at Kuanyeiji, and it is also said to have been intended for emergencies like the present. Having seized upon the person of Rinnôji no Miya, these seditious persons thought they could devise something. The *Shittô* Gakuô-In pretended to be perfectly qualified to judge of right conduct and duty, and taking upon himself to find fault with the late proceedings of the Imperial

---

(60) This was a temporary office, created for the moment. It would be translated censor in China, but as there is no real English equivalent it is best to retain the native term.

(61) The name of the park at Uyéno which contains the cemeteries of several of the Tokugawa Shôguns. It is also called Kuanyeiji.

Court, completely deceived the Miya, and obtained his sanction to the doings of the seditious ones. The Aidzu clan and *samurai* belonging to other clans of the Kuantô assisted with their moral support, and the seditious gained confidence. They invited men to enlist and repaired their arms. Many of the runaway troops, who had been hiding in Yedo since their defeat, and low fellows who were out of employment, spread the news and came to join, in hopes of filling their bellies for the moment. There is no law or order amongst a heterogeneous body of this sort (lit. a collection of tiles, an assemblage of rooks). When they walked forth for amusement they carried long swords in their girdles, wore high clogs, put on the airs of swashbucklers, and swaggered as much as possible. The loyal troops wore a piece of brocade sewn on to their clothes as a mutual sign, and the inhabitants of the city used to ridicule them in secret, calling them 'shreds of brocade' *(Kingiré)*. If the *Shôgitai* met with a 'shred of brocade' in the streets, they immediately heaped all manner of insults upon him, or attacked and killed him with their swords. A large number of loyal soldiers were murdered in this way. The townspeople all feared the prowess of the *Shôgitai*, who became highly elated, and the indignation of the troops of the various clans was so strong that they petitioned for leave to inflict chastisement. The Miya Commander-in-chief and the Kausasshi issued an order to the Tokugawa family to disband the troops collected at Tôyeizan, but the *Shôgitai* refused to obey. The Imperial court then summoned Rinnôji no Miya, with the object of reasoning with him, but Gakuô-In interfered, and prevented him from attending. It then became necessary for the Court to issue orders for an attack to be made upon the *Shôgitai*. Ômura Masujirô, the chief director of Military Affairs, was taken into council, and it was he who assigned to the different divisions the points which they were to attack. Satsuma, Higo and Inshiu advanced from Yujima, Chôshiu, Hizen, Chikugo, Ômura and Sadowara from Hongô, and besides these Bizen, Tôdô, Awa, Owari, Kishiu, Geishiu, and Chikuzen had various posts given to them. The rebels having heard of the plans, several hundred of them profited by the night of the 3rd July to make their escape.

On the morning of the 4th, just as day was beginning to break, the loyal forces made a simultaneous advance upon Tôyeizen. The rebels had previously taken quantities of *saké*, and under its influence they made a vigorous charge out of the gate, which caused the loyal forces to retire on Hirokôji.[62] Under cover of a violent storm of rain and wind which prevailed at the time the latter fought with enthusiasm, and having finally made a breach at one corner of the Black Gate, put the rebels to fight. Gakuô-In and his friends were dismayed, and taking the Miya with them barely escaped with their lives by a bye-path, seeking concealment in the town. Another body of rebels had occupied Sannô Yama[63], whence they fired down on loyal forces. The troops of Satsuma and other clans thereupon climbed into the trees, and fired up at them. The bullets of the rebels fell like hail, and a large number of men were knocked over, but the loyal forces kept on bringing up fresh men, and succeeded at last in driving the rebels from their position. The rebels then occupied the *hondô* (Chief Hall) of the monastery, and endeavoured to defend themselves, but the loyal forces set it on fire, compelling them to escape in a body. The loyal forces at Nedzu and Dango zaka were lying in wait, and completely annihilated them. During this engagement most of the part of the town in the immediate vicinity of Tôyeizan fell a prey to the flames. The *hondô* continued to burn with increasing fierceness during the night, and the smoke and flames rose up to the sky; it was not till ten o'clock

---

(62) The wide street leading up to the main gate.
(63) An elevated spot in the grounds of Hiyeizen where stood a shrine to the Shintô daity Sannô.

at night that the conflagration ceased. Fear fell upon all men, and the inhabitants of the city, when they saw the 'shreds of brocade', communicated their awe to each other, so that the 'shreds of brocade,' at last commanded respect throughout Yedo. Shortly afterwards the Imperial Court fixed the amount of the Tokugawa fief. Seven hundred thousand *koku* of land in Suruga, Tôtômi, Ôshiu and Déwa were granted to the clan, while the retainers were deprived of their titles. Before the amount of the fief was determined the retainers of the Tokugawa family had expected that three million *koku* would be granted, or two million at least, so that when the decree was issued they were filled with consternation, and all said that the *Shôgitai* had really ruined the business.

Some time before this Hayashi Shônoské, in concert with the runaways, had departed to his fief at the head of several hundred men, and now occupied the pass of Hakoné. The Imperial Court despatched two of its Military Inspectors named Nakai and Mikumo to Odáwara, to attack Hayashi and his companions with the troops of that clan; but the Odawara people secretly aided Hayashi, and having killed Nakai, expelled Mikumo from the town. The Imperial Court immediately marched its armies against Odawara to demand satisfaction, to the great alarm of the clan, which found itself perfectly helpless. It put the ringleaders to death, and begged for mercy on the condition of attacking Hayashi and his companions, but the latter shortly afterwards escaped by sea to the north. The Imperial Court deprived Odawara of a portion of its territory, and pardoned its offence, after which the eight provinces of the Kuantô became quiet again.

During this month the Court announced to the Tokugawa family, that, as a special act of grace, it would take into its service the remaining retainers. This was followed by the submission of a large number of them.

Before this an expedition had been despatched to attack Aidzu. The troops of Kaga, Owari, Satsuma, Chôshiu, Echizen, Matsushiro and Matsumoto advanced from the Echigo side, while other detachments of Satsuma and Chôshiu, with the troops of Ôgaki and Oshi-no-Giôda, advanced by way of Shirakawa in Ôshiu. The runaway soldiers of Tokugawa, together with the troops of Aidzu, Sendai, Tanagura, Nakamura and other clans, had occupied the castle of Shirakawa, and defended their position with vigour. The loyal forces engaged them hotly, and, after experiencing an average loss in killed and wounded, succeeded in taking the place. This was followed by the general submission of the surrounding district. Shortly afterwards the rebel army attacked Shirakawa in great force, and defeating the loyal forces, occupied the castle.

About the same time some four hundred troops of the Mito clan, under the leadership of Ichikawa and Asaina, two of the 'wicked party,' joined the rebel army in Echigo. The rebels were in occupation of the Castle of Nagaoka, Ochiya and other places, and their strength was increasing daily; but the loyal forces attacked them at Ochiya and put them to flight. Detachments were then posted at various points, some on the opposite side of the Shinano gawa, while others held the Enoki pass, Miôken and Kanagura yama. The Enoki pass is very steep; on the left it commands the Shinano gawa, while on the right it lies close to Kanagura yama, in the direct road to Nagaoka. This pass had hitherto been occupied by the rebels, but they were expelled from it by the Matsushiro and Owari troops. The loyal forces then advanced on Nagaoka from all sides, but the rebels fought stoutly for several days in succession, without the victory declaring itself for either side. After an interval of ten days, the rebels surrounded Miôken and the Enoki pass in great force, which places were defended by the troops of Satsuma, Chôshiu, Owari and Uyéda. The loyal forces on the eastern bank of the river, being thus cut off from their supports, were left alone in a position of great peril. The Military Counsellors Kuroda Riôsuké and Yamagata Kiôské picked out the best men from the troops on the right bank, and sent them to fall upon the rebels in front and rear. Profiting by the morning mists the captains Miyoshi Guntarô, Hori Sentarô and Sakéda Jiuzaemon started in command of two hundred Chôshiu and Takata troops, 'with gags in their mouths,'⁶⁴ and crossed the river Chikuma gawa. Heavy rain had fallen for some weeks previously and the river was so swollen that the boats were nearly upset. The men had great difficulty in reaching the opposite bank, but landed without loss of time and attacked the rebel earthworks. Great confusion ensued, and the rebels hastily abandoned their position. The loyal forces then took possession of the artillery, and turned it on the rebels, several tens of whom fell. At the same moment three hundred men of the Satsuma and other clans crossed from Uyéshita mura, took a rebel redoubt, and put the occupants to flight. The rest of the forces then crossed the river, and the loyal troops from the Enoki pass and Miôken also hastening up, the rebel army fell into great confusion. The loyal troops then advanced simultaneously with drums beating, and the rebels, after burning the Castle, retreated to Tochio by a byeroad, taking the *daimiô* of Nagaoka with them. The loyal army occupied the town at noon.

Upon the news of the reverse at Shirakawa being brought to Yedo the Imperial Court despatched the troops of Inshiu, Bizen, Ômura, Yanagawa, Sadowara and Kasama as reinforcements, and upon their arrival joint attack was made by the whole army. The rebels were dismayed, and throwing down their arms took to flight. In the 6th month (July 20—Aug. 17) the castle was at

---

(64) This is a Chinese metaphor, not warranted by Japanese practice.

last retaken by the loyal forces. The road to Shirakawa being very hilly the possession of the place carried with it great advantages both for offence and defence, and it was on this account that the two armies contested it so hotly.

Having thus taken the castle of Shirakawa, the loyal forces proceeded to strengthen its defences, with the object of advancing on Aidzu with the least possible delay. The rebels on their side being strongly posted at the castles of Tanagura and Iwakidaira, they then separated into two divisions, one of which advanced by way of Hata, while the other took the high road. About daybreak on the 12th August they closed in upon the castle of Tanagura, and after spending some time in bombarding it, captured it at two o'clock in the afternoon. The rebels thereupon concentrated their best troops at Iwakidaira, and they maintained such a bold front that the loyal army was almost unable to advance. In the seventh month (Aug. 18—Sept. 15) the Military Adviser Kawada Sakuma and his officers determined on a plan for making the attack with the combined forces of all the clans. The Inchiu, Yanagawa, Sadowara and Bizen troops advanced by Yumoto; another body of Yanagawa troops with those of Satsuma, Shôshiu and Ômura taking the Onahama road. Before dawn on the 30th August they approached Iwakidaira, but the rebels having obtained information beforehand, had left the castle and thrown up a battery about a *ri* distant. The Inshiu, Yanagawa, and other troops nevertheless attacked and put them to flight, after which they advanced towards the castle. The rebels had erected a stockade outside the gate and discharged a volley of musketry from behind it on the Yanagawa troops, but the latter made a spirited attack and forced their way in. The Satsuma troops also captured the outer ring of the castle. Still the rebels kept up an artillery fire from the other end of the bridge. A hundred and fifty Yanagawa men crept secretly along the beams which supported it and suddenly fell on the right wing of the rebels, while others of the loyal troops advanced along the bridge. The rebels now gave way and retreated into the keep, followed closely by the loyal forces, who attacked them in their stronghold. The defence was stout, and the thunder of the artillery resounded on all sides, enough to crumble heaven and earth into ruins. As night had come on, the loyal army withdrew to a secure position outside the castle, intending to renew the attack on the following day, but about twelve o'clock in the night flames burst out in the keep with great violence, and when the loyal forces hastened together to the spot, they could not find a single rebel soldier. During the fight of the previous day the rebels had resisted to the utmost of their strength, and had exhausted nearly all their powder; but before their resistance had lasted twelve hours the loyal forces had assembled on the outside of the castle. They recognized the consequent uselessness of trying to continue the defence, and therefore fled eastwards along the seashore-road, after setting fire to the castle. The loyal forces thus obtained command of the whole neighbourhood. Iwaki-daira is famed for having a stronger position than any other place in Ôshiu or Déwa; it is convenient to defend but difficult to attack. To this cause was ascribed the fact that the loyal forces lost more than the rebels in killed and wounded.

At this moment Ninnaji no Miya, accompanied by the two Court nobles Saionji and Mibu, was in Echigo at the head of the forces, having been appointed commander-in-Chief of the Expedition for the chastisement of Aidzu. The army occupied Nagaoka, and was engaged in throwing up earth works in the vicinity. On the side of the rebels also great activity was desplayed in the construction of fortifications close opposite, which were manned by runaway Tokugawa soldiers, and by the troops of the

Aidzu, Yonézawa, Nagaoka and other clans, and they completely blocked up the roads. Cannonading went on every day without any decisive result. A council of war was held by the loyal forces on the 10th of September, at which it was decided to break through the rebel lines and to march on Aidzu. The points at which each division was to attack were duly laid down, and as it had been reported that another division of the loyal forces had landed from a large war vessel somewhere in the territory of Shibata, the whole army lay down to take a slight sleep, with the intention of taking the field on the morrow at day-break. The rebels were however perfectly acquainted with this plan, and in the middle of the night they sent a body of picked troops to attack the most exposed earthworks. Profiting by the disorder created amongst the loyal troops by their vigorous musketry and artillery fire they advanced upon Nagaoka, the garrison of which, on hearing the sound of firing, supposed it to be a signal that their own side was attacking the rebels, and made ready to march. Soon fires burst out in all directions and the sound of firing gradually approached; and they were astounded when the scouts reported, saying: 'the rebel troops have advanced to the attack.' The rebels arrived immediately afterwards, and falling violently on the loyal troops, inflicted a severe defeat on them. Following up their advantage, they pursued the fugitives and hurled them into the river. A large number of the loyal troops were thus killed. Shortly afterwards the day broke, and the rebel troops succeeded in recovering Nagaoka. From the moment of the capture of this town by the loyal army the towns-people had been in constant communication with the rebel forces, and kept them daily informed of what went on in the loyal army, and on the occasion of this battle they had been particularly useful in this way, which was believed to be the cause of the marked success of the rebels.

On the 12th, one part of the loyal army collected at the Enoki pass and at Miôkenzaka, while the other occupied the left bank of the Shinano gawa. They busied themselves in constructing batteries on the edge of the river, and in fighting the rebels. The latter prepared to cross the river in great force and to come to close quarters, and the loyal army had great difficulty in maintaining its ground. Some proposed to retreat over the Mikuni pass in order to elude the rebels while they were fresh, and attack them when they became exhausted, but the military adviser Yamagata replied: "To retreat a single step " at the present junction would be simply encouraging " the rebels, while every step we take in advance dis- " concerts their plans. Why need we consider that " our strategy has failed because of a single reverse? " I am informed that the Shirakawa army has already " taken possession of the surrounding country and is daily " forcing its way further into Mutsu and Déwa. I am of " opinion that these slaves must look to their rear, and " that they cannot long hold out. Do you gentlemen " strive your hardest." A plan for renewing the attack was then determined on, while the rebels, rendered complacent by their victory of the previous day, were gradually relaxing their vigilance.

At day-break on the morning of the 15th the loyal forces profited by a dense fog to reconnoitre the rebel camp from Miôken, and ascertained that the rebels were still asleep. Upon this they drew their swords, and rushed in, hacking about them on all sides, and killing several tens of the rebels. They then poured in a vigorous fire with their muskets, and the blood of the defeated rebels dyed the earth. The loyal forces then appeared on all sides, and advanced on Nagaoka with shouts, throwing the rebels into complete confusion. Having fired the town in every quarter, they opened fire with the artillery, and the dismayed rebels fled out of the place, which the loyal army succeeded in occupying. Those of the inhabitants who had been in communication with the rebels were arrested without exception, and condemned to death. The town of Nagaoka had been so frequently fired by the soldiery since the fifth month (June 20—July 19) that the castle and streets had been almost entirely destroyed, leaving nothing but a wide and desolate waste.

During this month the name of Yedo was changed to Tôkiô.[65]

A short time before these events three commanders of the Aidzu expedition, namely the Court nobles Kujô, Sawa and Daigo, had proceeded by different roads into Mutsu and Déwa, accompanied by eighty Satsuma and Chôshiu soldiers, to assume the direction of the clans in those provinces, but most of the clans mistrusted them, and they were unable to enforce their orders. The troops of Akita, Tsugaru and Ikoma alone obeyed them. When the Aidzu clan first withdrew to its territory, it commenced making preparations for war, and the prince of Shônai also gave orders to his clan to give secret moral support to Aidzu. The Akita and Ikoma troops consequently had several encounters with Shônai, in which they were usually defeated. Shortly afterward the runaway Tokugawa soldiers, in combination with deserters from Sendai and the Shônai troops, invaded the territory of Akita, which complained to Kujô, who, with Daigo, was at this moment at Sendai. The Sendai and Yonégawa clans, on receiving orders to join the expedition against Aidzu, had despatched troops to the frontier, where they received letters from Aidzu imploring their pity. They consequently withdrew their troops, and having assembled

---

(65) Or Tôkei, another pronunciation. It is possible that this change, apparently so unnecessary, was made in order to facilitate the Mikado's removal from Kiôto, by familiarizing the people with the idea of two capitals, an eastern and a western one. Though the name Kiôto has been retained as the official designation of the ancient residence of the sovereign, it is more often called Saikiô, or Western capital, by all classes, in contradistinction to Tôkiô, thus proving that the object, if there was one, has been attained.

a conference at Shiraishi of Nambu, Niwa, Miharu and seven other clans, entered into a league, the object of which was to obtain the pardon of Aidzu, as set forth in a joint petition which they addressed to Kujô. The Military Counsellors replied: "If Aidzu sincerely wished to " beg pardon for his offence, he would give material proof " of submissiveness by surrendering his castle and hand-" ing over his arms. But instead of acting thus, he has " detached troops to the castles in the neighbourhood, and " is straining even now to strengthen his defences, thus " offering resistance to the Loyal Army. At the same " time he sends in letters, palliating his errors and im-" ploring pity. Is this the proper way to ask pardon for " offences? And do the clans consider this right? We " have also heard that *samurai* of the Sendai and other " clans have secretly joined the rebel army in large numbers." They therefore rejected the letter without taking any notice of it, and gave orders to march the troops against Aidzu. Sendai, Yonézawa and the other clans were decidedly unwilling to obey, and the seditious clansmen grew angry, saying: "The generals were willing to " grant our request, but the Military advisers have inter-" fered and prevented their doing so. They make use of " the Imperial Court as a tool for the execution of their " own schemes, and their treasonable practices will be " punished as they deserve." They then assassinated the Military adviser Serata, and published a list of the crimes of which they accused him, in order to stir up Nambu and the other clans to resistance. Great excitement was the result, and the clans took counsel together to aid Aidzu in concert. The commotion spread far and wide. Kujô and his companions thereupon quitted Sendai and came to Morioka, but as this clan had joined the league, the soldiers carried off Kujô and Daigo, and took refuge in Akita, where they found Sawa. Having consulted together they despatched a secret messenger to Yedo with information of the alarming state of affairs. The Imperial Court was profoundly alarmed. All the *daimiôs* of Mutsu and Déwa were deprived of their titles, and orders having been issued to chastise them, troops were moved forward in increasing numbers. Rinnôji no Miya and Gakuô-In, who had absconded some time before, were in the north, and they now entered Sendai, where they were acknowledged by the clan. The confederated clans became more confident, and breaking off all relations with the loyal army, at last advanced upon Akita. This clan, left entirely to itself, was in imminent danger of being defeated and crushed, but the troops of Satsuma, Tosa, Hizen, Shimabara and Hirado arrived shortly afterwards, and the loyal army recovered its strength in a great measure. Kujô and the others, finding themselves surrounded by enemies and obliged to wander about and undergo all sorts of hardships, had been in a very uncomfortable position, so that they now felt as if they had been restored to life.

The loyal army in Akita, being now recruited, daily made excursions into the neighbourhood, which consequently had to submit. The other divisions also daily advanced further into the enemy's territory, and captured both Nihommatsu and Miharu. The troops of Sendai, Nambu, Yonézawa and Shônai made an obstinate resistance, but the loyal army, after some hard fighting, succeeded in taking Komagaminé in the Sendai territory. At the same time detachments were sent by the different divisions to attack Nambu, Yonézawa and Shônai, but the rebels resisted so sturdily that the loyal army met with frequent reverses. But not long afterwards the rebels began to feel disheartened at the defeats which they had sustained in Echigo and at Shirakawa, while the loyal army was everywhere triumphant, and began to close in upon Sendai and the other three clans.

In the eighth month (September 16—October 15) Kayô no Miya was deprived of his patent of nobility. This

Prince, who harboured schemes of his own, had been in communication with the Kuantô from the time of Tokugawa Keiki's flight to the east, and had sent secret messengers to him. Keiki, however, rejected his overtures, and returned no answer. When the Prince's intrigues were discovered, he was banished to Geishiu. Kayô no Miya is the same person as the In no Miya.

During Keiki's residence in Mito fighting continued to go on in the immediate vicinity, and it was falsely rumoured that the seditious intended to seize his person; so that he had reason to fear new complications. The retainers of the Tokugawa family being now settled on the fief in Suruga, Keiki sent in a memorial, praying for leave to remove to Sumpu, and the Imperial Court granted his request. He at once removed thither, and remained there in strict seclusion.

During this month Enomoto Kamajirô, Matsudaira Tarô and Arai Ikunoské, with Nagai Gemba at their head, carried off the Kaijô, Kaiten, Banriu, Shinsoku, Chôkei, Oyé and Hôgô, seven vessels in all, from the Shinagawa anchorage. The Imperial Court had at first intended to take possession of all the war-vessels belonging to the Tokugawa family, but Enomoto and his friends petitioned to be allowed to keep them, so that the Court was obliged to be content with the Fujiyama and three others, bestowing the Kaiyô Maru and the rest upon the Tokugawa family. Enomoto was a skilled navigator, and the officers under his command were also experienced in their profession. The Kaiyô Maru, of which he was captain, carried twenty-six guns, and the engines were of 400 horsepower; she was solidly constructed and well-equipped, and had the reputation of being the finest vessel in Japan. Presuming on the possession of such a ship, the naval men had constantly found fault with the submissiveness of the chief of the clan. When the Drilled Troops deserted from Yedo, Enomoto, who happened to be lying off Shinagawa, secretly entered into combination with them, and they promised to assist each other when the opportunity should arrive. When he and his companions heard of the rising of the confederated clans in Mutsu and Déwa they took counsel together, saying: "Who in the empire can resist "us, being in command of such powerful war-vessel? It "will be perfectly easy for us to roam at will over the "sea, and lend aid to the land forces." So they sent in a letter to the Court, in which the necessity of pacifying the crews was given as the pretext for leaving, and then departed. The Tokugawa family sent a despatch-vessel in pursuit, but being unable to evertake them, handed in the letter to the Imperial Court. The Court was violently angry, and severely censured the Tokugawa family for the haughty and insolent language of the document. The Tokugawa family was at its wit's end. The Court then declared Enomoto and his companions to be pirates, and in communicating this to the representatives of foreign countries, desired them to hold no communication with the ships. A proclamation was also issued to the people, interdicting them from furnishing supplies to the runaway vessels.

By this time the loyal army, having occupied Nihommatsu, was attacking Sendai and the other clans with separate detachments. It advanced every day further into the enemy's territory, but without taking any notice of Aidzu. The Aidzu clan and the runaway soldiers held all the roads in that district, and continued strengthening their position. The Military advisers Ijichi and Itagaki took counsel together, saying: " Aidzu is the root of the "rebellion, while Sendai and the other clans are but the "leaves and branches. If we pursue the leaves and "branches, and neglect the root, they will spring up again "as often as we destroy them. The best plan would be "to disturb the root, for if that once moves, the leaves "and branches will wither of themselves. Besides, thirty "days from this the castle of Wakamatsu will be deep in "snow, and the cold will be so intense that the army will "be unable to advance. We must lose no time." So leaving the other clans to act against Sendai and its confederates, they started from Nihommatsu on the 7th of October at the head of the Satsuma, Chôshiu, Tosa, Ôgaki and Ômura troops, and marched in the direction of the Katanari pass, which forms the boundary between the fiefs of Aidzu and Nihommatsu. The rebels had previously constructed a battery on the summit of the pass, and as the troops advanced they opened fire. The loyal forces put them to flight in the first engagement, and captured Inawashiro on the same day. Having constructed a temporary bridge in place of the bridge at the side of the lake, which the rebels had destroyed in order to stop the way, they crossed the river, and routed the troops which were stationed on the Takizawa pass. On the 8th, they entered pell-mell into the town of Wakamatsu, and straightway took the outer ring of the castle. The rebels were taken by surprise, and said: "Has "the loyal army flown here?" and retired within the castle in a body. The Aidzu clan had stationed large bodies of troops at Aidzugawa, Shônai, Fujiwara, Sandogoya and other passes to meet the attack of the loyal army, and trusting to the precipitous character of the Inawashiro pass had only detached a few tens to that place, so that the loyal army, profiting by their weakness at this point, quite took the rebels aback. Advancing upon the town, it bombarded the castle day after day, so as to crush the spirit of the rebels, and give time for the remaining divisions to come up. When the rebel detachments who were scattered about to hold the other passes heard that the loyal army had entered the town of Wakamatsu they abandoned their posts and fled to the castle.

Early on the morning of the 10th the garrison sallied

forth in great numbers and attacked the loyal forces, defeating them completely and killing many. The military advisers therefore dispersed their troops for a while, and the rebels, not venturing to follow them up, retired into the castle. The loyal army then reassembled, but was a second time routed by the garrison, who attacked it about noon. At the same moment, however, a detachment of the loyal army fell upon the rear of the rebels and created great confusion. This enabled it to rally and inflict a severe defeat on the garrison, which retreated into the castle.

On the same day the troops of Owari, Kishiu, Hizen, etcetera, advancing from Shirakawa, and those of Geishiu, Utsunomiya, Ôtawara, etcetera advancing from Fujiwara, attacked the rebel troops whom they encountered on their line of march, and entered the town of Wakamatsu by dusk. At twelve o'clock at night the garrison stealthily assaulted the camp of the loyal army, which repulsed them after some hard fighting. These nocturnal sorties became henceforth matters of frequent occurrence, and the loyal army had hard work to defend itself.

At this moment the loyal army in Echigo advanced upon Aidzugawa with the object of entering Wakamatsu. The rebels had constructed a line of posts twenty miles in length on the opposite side of the river, which the loyal forces, after some desperate fighting, succeeded in turning. But the rebels put forth all their strength, and fought so hard that they managed to keep the road effectually barred. Shortly afterwards the loyal army which was at Wakamatsu advanced upon the rebels at Aidzu-gawa, and drew off their attention, thus giving the loyal army of Echigo an opportunity, of which it availed itself to defeat the rebels. The latter therefore abandoned their positions and reached the castle of Wakamatsu by bye-roads. On the 25th October the whole of the loyal army of Echigo entered the town of Wakamatsu, and effected a junction with the other divisions. The loyal army was therefore in great force. That division of it which had advanced from Nihommatsu had captured Tenneiji yama, close to the castle in a commanding position. Field pieces were at once placed in position and a cannonade directed upon the interior of the fortress. The garrison defended themselves stoutly, and replied to the fire, so that the loyal forces found it necessary to construct another battery over against the southeast corner of the castle, from which they kept up a vigorous bombardment.

On the night of the 28th the garrison made a sortie in force to the east of the castle and surprised the loyal army, which, owing to its ignorance of the locality, was defeated and dispersed, with great loss both in killed and wounded. On the following morning the loyal army bombarded the castle with shell, hitting the towers and keep with destructive effect. A large number of the garrison were killed by the fragments, and the inmates of the castle were aghast. Nevertheless the garrison flew kites over the castle, in order to convey the idea that they had plenty of leisure for amusement. Not long afterwards the division which lay on the west of the castle pressed up and cannonaded it, but the garrison replied with such effect as to lay many of the loyal troops low.

On the 30th the whole army made a combined advance on the castle, thus preventing the garrison from making any more sorties. The Military Advisers Ijichi, Yamagata and Itagaki took counsel together, saying: "When " an army advances far from its base into a mountainous ": country, and continues this long, calamities are not un- " likely to befall it. The best plan would be to assault " the castle boldly, scaling in it a body, and so settle the " question of victory or defeat." They then assigned to each division the point at which it should make the attack.

The duty of leading the van was imposed upon the Yonézawa clan, which had lately given in its adhesion to the loyal army. It consequently set its troops in motion, and the garrison, henceforth deprived of its moral support, was considerably weakened. In the confusion consequent upon the entrance of the loyal army from Nihommatsu, the rebels had been unable to put the castle in a complete state of defence, and their provisions were already exhausted. Moreover, the Sendai and other clans, disheartened by repeated reverses, were on the point of offering their submission and praying for pardon.

On the 3rd of November Téshirogi and Akidzuki of the Aidzu clan sent a messenger to the Yonézawa camp, the occupants of which, afraid of incurring suspicion, bound him and sent him to the Tosa camp. On being interrogated by the Tosa troops, he explained that the garrison wished to surrender. After consulting together, the Military advisers granted the following conditions, namely that the prince and his son should come and surrender themselves, and that the castle, together with the arms, should be handed over, by a certain day. They then dismissed the messenger. The Aidzu clan accepted the conditions.

On the 7th the prince, his son and their principal retainers came forth from the castle and surrendered, offering possession of the castle and the arms at the same time. It is said that a certain principal retainer of the clan, humiliated by this result, slew his wife and children, and killed himself by falling on his sword. Five days later Sendai, Nambu, Shônai and the other clans submitted, and gave up their arms. The Nambu clan subsequently revolted again, but was subdued by the loyal army in a single engagement.

Shortly before this, when the fall of Wakamatsu became imminent, Ichikawa and Asaina, members of the Wicked Party in Mito, entered that town with several hundred of their associates, but the Righteous Party resisted them, and many were killed or wounded on either side. The Righteous party then reported the affair to the Imperial Court, which despatched the clans of the vicinity to chastise the Wicked Party. They were severely defeated, and Asaina and Ichikawa, barely escaping with their lives, sought a hiding place in the neighbourhood of Narita in Shimôsa, but being discovered and arrested by the Mito clan, suffered death by decapitation.

When the loyal army attacked the castle of Wakamatsu, it was only provided with twelve-pounder guns, the larger cannon being too heavy for transport on account of the hilly nature of the surrounding country. It was this cause which lengthened out the siege of a single fortress by so large a force to thirty days. When the Eastern war broke out the clans of Mutsu and Déwa were all armed with ordinary muskets, while the loyal army opposed them with breechloaders of American invention, which was the cause of their being so terrible in fight.

On the 22nd of this month (Nov. 6) no capital punishments were inflicted in any part of the Empire, it being the Tennô's birthday, and he entertained all his officials with a banquet. Henceforward the day was constituted the Imperial Fête, and the whole empire was commanded to celebrate it as an occasion for rejoicing. The chronological period was also changed to Meiji (Enlightened Government), and an imperial proclamation was published making it a rule for all time that there should be only one chronological period for each reign.

During the spring of this year the Gazette *Dajôkan nisshi* was printed, and published to the empire, so that all the people might be acquainted with the administrative decrees.

During the summer of this year government paper money was manufactured, in consequence of the expenditure being in excess of the revenue. It was first placed in circulation in the following spring.

A treaty was concluded with Spain in the autumn. Englishmen were hired to build lighthouses at various points on the coast, so as to facilitate the navigation of the seas.

On the 16th November [66] the Tennô arrived in Tôkiô. Arisugawa, the Miya Commanding-in-Chief, returned into his hands the brocade banner and the sword of justice (settô) in token of the pacification of the north and east. His Majesty graciously thanked him for his services, and bestowed gifts of money on the other military officers. He then ordered all his officials to discuss the sentences to be passed on the clans of Mutsu, Déwa and Echigo which had given in their submission.

In the 11th month (December 14—January 12 1869), the Prince of Aidzu and his son and the Princes of Sendai, Yonézawa and the other clans were summoned to Tôkiô. Shortly afterwards Rinnôji no Miya and his following returned from the north. He was placed in seclusion in the Palace of Fushimi no Miya at Saikiô (Kiôtô). Itakura Iga and his son, and the other runaway leaders, also returned and were placed in seclusion.

1869.—In the 12th month (January 13—February 10) a special Imperial Proclamation was published condemning the Princes of Aidzu, Sendai, Yonézawa and other clans to punishment one degree less than death, and to seclusion in their several clans. The territories of Sendai, Yonézawa and the rest were all diminished by one-third, and the succession to those fiefs given to a member of each family. The province of Mutsunoku (Mutsu, or Ôshiu) was divided into five, namely Iwaki, Iwashiro, Rikuzen, Rikuchiu and Mutsunoku. Déwa was divided into two provinces, Uzen and Ugo. In the following year lands at Tonami in Mutsu, assessed at 30,000 *koku* of rice, were bestowed on the Hoshina family, in order that

---

(66) This is an error for November 26th.

its ancestral sacrifices[67] might be kept up. The troubles of the Empire were now nearly at an end.

During the month an imperial order was given to Iwakura Uhiôyei no kami to persuade the representatives of England, France, America, Holland, Italy and Prussia, to withdraw their neutrality notifications, and he gave them a letter, saying: "The rebellious clans of "Mutsu, Déwa and Echigo have now asked for pardon "and have given in their submission. The chiefs of "those clans have come to Tôkiô and are looking for the "decision of the government. There is therefore no clan "in the country which opposes the Government, and no "objection can exist either to selling or lending war- "vessels and arms to my government. I pray you to "consent to this." After several days consultation the representatives issued notifications to their subjects by which the neutrality was abolished. The Tennô then returned to Saikiô.

Through the withdrawal of the neutrality notifications by the foreign countries our Government was for the first time enabled to obtain possession of an ironclad. This ironclad had been purchased by the Tokugawa family from America and had arrived at Yokohama during the summer of the year 1868. Upon its arrival the Government had desired to take it over, but the Americans hoisted their flag on it, and because of the neutrality proclamation refused to give it up. When the neutrality came to an end, the Government persuaded them to give

---

(67) If Shintô is a genuine product of Japanese soil, then the custom of sacrificing to ancestors might fairly be termed its origin and essence; but it is difficult not to suspect the latter of being of Chinese origin, like so many of the customs which are usually regarded as native. The practice of adoption, which supplies the childless with heirs, is common all over the east, but its justification in Japan is the necessity of keeping up the ancestral sacrifices; in the case of the prince of Aidzu this necessity is the pretext for not driving the clan to extremities by reducing it to absolute beggary. Hoshina was the original family name of the princes of Aidzu, but they were permitted to bear that of Matsudaira as distant relatives of the Tokugawa Shôguns. After the fall of Keiki, all those princes who had borne this fictitious surname discarded it, some from choice, others because they were compelled to do so.

it up. The Kaiyô Maru had been looked upon as the finest war-vessel in Japan, but when the ironclad arrived it was considered by some the better of the two.

When the clans of the north and east all gave in their submission, Enomoto Kamajirô and his friends, who were in the Sendai territory with the war vessels, found themselves deprived of shelter. Ôtori Keiské also retreated from Aidzu at the head of the runaway troops, and fleeing to Sendai, sought shelter with the marine army. Hereupon, after consulting together, they resolved to seize upon Hakodaté as a base for their operations. Having quitted Sendai, they came to the port of Washinoki, distant about ten *ri* from Hakodaté. Shimidzu-dani Jijiu, the Governor of Hakodaté, was at the fort of Kaméda, and protected it by stationing a few tens of Sataké, Tsugaru, Matsumaë, Ôno, Ogura and Fukuyama troops at various points, but on hearing of the approach of the runaway vessels, he quitted the fort and retired into the town. He eventually retired to Awomori in Tsugaru, and despatched the *Sanji* (Vice-Governor) Hori Shingorô to Tôkiô to give the alarm. The rebel army shortly afterwards landed at Washinoki and separated into two bodies, one of which was directed against Hakodaté under the command of Ôtori Keiské, while the other advanced to Tôgéshita, but being attacked by the loyal army at the village of Ôno, was forced to retreat. On hearing of this Ôtori Keiské sent fresh troops to their aid, and the loyal army was finally routed.

At the same time a rebel leader named Hijikata Saizô started from Washinoki in command of other troops, and crossing the Kawasui pass, arrived at Hakodaté by a bye-road. He then sent out detachments to scour the country, and occupied the villages of Ôno and Fumidzuki. The troops of Fukuyama and other clans opposed them at Nanaë, and inflicted a severe defeat on them, but not long afterwards the rebel army came back in great force to fight. The loyal army fought bravely, and killed Ôoka and Suwaté, two rebel captains, but the rebels were not dismayed, and after several hard-fought engagements severely defeated the loyal army, which lost heavily in killed and wounded. Encouraged by their success, the rebels then proceeded to capture the fort at Kaméda, and two of the runaway vessels, namely the Kuaiten and Banriu, came round from the harbour of Washinoki to Hakodaté. The loyal troops had previously retired to Awomori with the governor, so that the town was entirely undefended, and the rebels had only to land and take possession. The Kaiyô and other war vessels now removed from Washinoki to Hakodaté, and the rebels electing Nagai Gemba to be their temporary chief, made him governor of the town. They informed the foreign residents of this arrangement and promised that he should settle all business affairs with them. At the same time the rebel marine forces put to sea in the Banriu, and advancing along the straits of Tsugaru [68], closed in upon the castle of Matsumaë. The Matsumaë troops fired upon the Banriu from the forts, and the rebels, manœuvring the vessel within the port, responded with shell. They destroyed one of the shore batteries, but the firing from the others redoubled, and solid shot constantly struck the runaway vessel, which, being unable to get in close to the castle, finally departed. The rebel land forces then advanced in conjunction with the ships: the marine army came to the bay of Fukushima and opened fire, while the land army under the leadership of Ôtori and Hijikata closed in upon the castle of Matsumaë by way of the villages of Fukushima and Ôno.

With the object of enabling the clansmen to maintain an obstinate defence, the prince had proceeded to Esashi, but the captain Yasuda Setsuzô and his son, aware that they

---

(68) Called Shiratsu Nada in the original.

would be unable to resist successfully, advised the prince to remove to another province. When other clansmen named Suzuki Oritarô and Tazaki Adzuma etc. heard of this, they were enraged at what seemed to them a love of inglorious ease, and proceeding to Esashi, attacked and slew Yasuda and his son. A commotion ensued in the clan, by which the rebels profited to enter the castle straightway. Tamura Riôkichi and others of the garrison set the castle on fire, and died in its defence. Thus the castle of Matsumaë fell into the hands of the rebels. Five days only had elapsed since the first attack, and the loss of the clan killed and wounded had been considerable.

Having thus taken Matsumaë, the rebel naval and military forces proceeded to concert measures for the reduction of Esashi and Taté. One division of the land forces advanced along the highroad from the castle, while the other took a bye-road from the fort at Kaméda. Enomoto and his companions, embarked in the Kaiyô Maru, had already arrived at the head of the naval force in the bay of Matsumaë, whence they sailed along the coast, and anchored before Esashi. The prince of Matsumaë and seventy followers had previously quitted Esashi and retired to Tsugaru. The naval force thereupon landed, and occupying the town, waited the arrival of the land army. In the night the wind and waves became very violent, and the Kaiyô Maru almost parted from her moorings. The rebels put on more steam, with the object of getting out to sea, so as to avoid the rocks; but the gale continued to increase, tossing the vessel about violently until she suddenly touched a hidden rock, and became perfectly unmanageable. The rebels were completely dismayed, and the commanders at Hakodaté, on hearing of the accident, despatched the Kuaiten and Shiusoku to bring aid, but the unabated force of the gale prevented the two vessels from approaching. In fact they barely contrived to turn round and get away. Enomoto and his companions remained on board the Kaiyô Maru for four days, when the wind abated a little, and they were enabled to land with their arms. Ten days later the ship became a perfect wreck, and the rebels felt like one who has lost his lantern on a dark night.

The loyal forces were still in possession of the barriers of Osunago and Inakuraishi, and the fort of Taté, but the rebel leader Hijikata advanced at the head of several hundred men, and beating them in a single fight, crossed the hills of Osunago, whence the tide of victory carried him right up to Esashi. The other rebel division, which was advancing along a bye-road, captured the barriers at Inakuraishi, and immediately closed in upon the fort at Taté. The loyal army closed the gates, and discharged vollies of musketry and cannon balls, while the rebels, who had been unable to carry any artillery over the mountain paths, could only advance under cover of a musketry fire. Suddenly two rebels came running up, and crawling under the gate, threw it open from the inside, and admitted their friends, who pressed in pellmell with loud yells. The loyal army resisted vigorously, and the ranks were thrown into such confusion that it became impossible to distinguish friends from foes. A loyal soldier named Mikami Chôjiun, brandishing his sword in his right hand and carrying a fishmonger's chopping-block in his left, engaged the rebel captain Ina Seichirô and cut him down on the spot. A rebel captain named Yokoda, who saw this, came running up with a pistol in his hand, and was likewise cut down by Mikami. Upon this two rebel soldiers ran up, and pierced Mikami through the body from behind so that he died. The loyal army having by this time been completely defeated, the rebels captured the fort, and advanced along the high-road, where they fell in with the other division. Having effected a junction they reached Kunnaishi, which they found deserted by the loyal troops. On this the rebel army returned to the fort at Kaméda, and a volley of blank cartridges was fired from the men-of-war and the batteries by way of a salute in honour of their having taken possession of the surrounding country. Enomoto shortly afterwards had an interview with the foreign consuls resident at Hakodaté and the captain of the English and French men-of-war, and informed them that he would decide all matters of business which might arise in the port. The captains of the English and French men-of-war sought to place him at his ease with smiling words, saying that they would act as mediators, and persuade our government to withdraw their troops. Enomoto thanked them for their generous sentiments, and prepared a letter in which he proposed to get a scion of the Tokugawa family to come among them, in order that they might develope the resources of Yezo and 'keep the key of the northern gate.' He entrusted this to the captains for delivery to the Government. The rebel troops were then ordered to appoint their chiefs by ballotting publicly for them. The result of the election was that Enomoto Kamajirô was chosen Governor-general (*Sôsai*), Matsudaira Tarô Assistant Governor-general (*Fuku-sôsai*), Arai Ikunoské Commissioner of the Navy (*Kaigun bugiô*) and Ôtori Keiské Military Commissioner (*Rikugun bugiô*). This was done in imitation of the practice observed in the United States of America, where these things are settled by the wish of the majority. The fort at Kaméda was constituted the head quarters, and governors (*bugiô*) were placed at Hakodaté, Matsumaë and Esashi, to superintend local affairs. With a view to the development of Yezo they removed two hundred men to Mororan, and appointed one Takézawa governor of that place.

As soon as the Imperial Court heard that the runaway vessels had taken Hakodaté it ordered the Tokugawa family to inflict chastisement, and Tokugawa Keiki prayed that he might go in person to chastise them. This the Court refused, and gave the order instead to the prince of

Mito. When the Court, therefore, read 'Enomoto's letter it was more than ever displeased at the insolence of his conduct, and issued orders to the whole Empire to chastise the runaway vessels. The rebels had already lost the Kaiyō Maru, and their military strength was correspondingly reduced, while the Government possessed the ironclad, and its naval forces were more formidable.

In the first month of the second year of Meiji (Feb. 11 —Mar. 12, 1869) the *daimiôs* of the home provinces and the western part of the country attended at Court to congratulate the Emperor on the occasion of the new year. On the 15th of February the Counsellor (*sanyo*) Yokoi Heishirô was attacked and murdered by some *ronins* on his way home from the Palace. No one knew the motive of this deed, but some said that the opponents of the constitutional changes which he constantly advocated had falsely charged him with professing evil opinions,[69] and the *rônins*, believing this, had acted in consequence. The *rônins* who had plotted this crime were afterwards arrested and decapitated, their heads being publicly exposed after their execution.

During this month it was prohibited to clear the road for the Nobles, to shout out ' Shitaniro' or otherwise to affect an empty dignity.

In the second month (March 13th—April 11th) a 'place of public debate' (*Kôgisho*) was established, and *samurai* of all the clans were appointed members (*gi-in*), with leave to discuss at their own discretion the means of governing. It name was afterwards changed to 'College of discussion in assembly' (*Shiugi-In*). This was carrying out the proposal made in 1868 of establishing meetings for discussion on a large scale, and of deciding upon all measures by impartial arguments.

During the same month the barriers which had heretofore existed at Hakoné and other places on the high-

(69) i.e. Christianity.

roads were abolished in order to facilitate travelling. Permission to print newspapers was accorded shortly afterwards. The punishments of transfixing with spears and death by burning were also abolished.

In the third month (April 12th—May 11th) the *Taishô-In* was established for the reception of memorials from *samurai* and the general population. It was afterwards made subordinate to the *Shiugi-In*.

In the same month the Tennô again visited Tôkiô. The Court nobles (*kugé*) and *daimiôs* had been previously summoned thither also, and they now assembled round the throne. The Imperial Court asked their opinion as to the basis of the principles of Government; this was also seeking after impartial discussion. They were shortly afterwards dismissed from attendance, but the Tennô prolonged his stay at Tôkiô, which was regarded by the people as the sign of an intention to transfer the capital thither.

In view of the projected expedition against Hakodaté the Imperial Court now notified the representatives of foreign countries to cause the subjects of those countries to remove from the port, and the sea and land forces were put in motion. The Imperial troops of Fushimi and the troops of the Hakodaté Fu, as well as those of the Satsuma, Higo, Chôshiu, Bizen, Mito, Tôdô, Kurumô, Fukuyama, Hirosaki, Matsumaë, Tokuyama, Ono and Kuroishi clans, amounting to about 6,500 men, started on different days in the direction of Hakodaté. As for the naval forces Shinagawa Yomoichi, Hijikata Kenkichi, Akatsuka Genroku, Nakamuta Kuranoské, Oka Seisaburô, Ishikawa Teinojô, Yamagata Kiutarô and others commanded the iron-clad, the Kasuga (Keangsoo), Teibô, Yôshun and other war-vessels.

Of these the ironclad, the Kasuga, Teibô, Yôshun and three others were the first to leave, and they betook themselves to the harbour of Miyako in Nambu. When the rebels heard of this they began to discuss how they might best resist the expedition, and Arai Ikunoské left Hakodaté with the Kuaiten, Banriu and Takao. On the 29th of April, before dawn, a war vessel arrived, braving the billows and flying American colours. The ships imagined it to be a foreign vessel, and therefore paid no attention, but the strange vessel, on finding that the others were unprepared, suddenly hoisted the national flag, discharged its guns, and bore down upon the ironclad. The ships then perceived for the first time that it was the Kuaiten, and immediately lit the fires under their boilers, but they were unable either to manœuvre or to work their guns. Ôtsuka, Nomura and other rebels took advantage of this to draw their swords and leap on board the ironclad, but Shinagawa, Hijikata, Waki and other loyal soldiers brandished their pikes, and straightway laid the rebels low. Kôga Gengo, the captain of the rebel ship, who was sitting on the bridge of the Kuaiten, gave orders to discharge a fifty-pounder gun, and the shot struck the deck of the iron-clad, wounding a number of loyal soldiers. The shots of the combined fleet now began to shower down upon the runaway vessel, while Kôga, manœuvring his ship backwards and forwards, responded to their fire. Some of the loyal troops took aim at the rebel captain with small-arms, hitting him in the left thigh and right arm, but Kôga was not to be daunted, and continued to cheer on his men. At last they contrived to lay him low, upon which the rebel soldiers lost heart, and suddenly quitted the harbour. The fleet pursued, but could not come up with the fugitive, whose object had apparently been the capture of the ironclad. It is said that the naval laws permit a vessel to enter a port flying the flag of another country, and after opening fire to hoist its own national flag, which proceeding was imitated by the Kuaiten on this occasion.

The Kuaiten set out on this expedition accompanied by the Banrin and Takao, but the two last named vessels

were separated from her by stress of weather and driven
out to sea. An accident occurred to the Takao's engines,
and she found herself close to the harbour of Miyako
unable to go ahead. The Captain, one Kikkawa, and his
crew of seventy men, after setting the ship on fire, landed in the Nambu territory and surrendered to the Morioka clan. The burning vessel was espied by the fleet as it
was pursuing the Kuaiten, but on nearing her, it was perceived that the flames had reached the hold and that she
was quite deserted; so the fleet left her and quitted the
spot. After this the fleet entered into a compact to advance straight upon Hakodaté. The rebels therefore detached the Kuaiten, Banriu and Chioda to crnise round
the harbour of Hakodaté day and night, to watch over its
safety. They also placed detachments of troops at the
Kaméda fort, at Hakodaté, Matsumaë, Esashi, Fukushima,
Mororan and other places, and then notified the foreign
residents that they must withdraw. The foreigners then
embarked on board the war vessels of their respective
nationalities and departed.

The Chôyô and other men-of-war arrived in the north
during the fourth month (May 12—June 9), and on the
12th of May weighed anchor from Awomori in Tsugaru
in company with the ironclad, the Kasuga, Yôshun,
Teibô and the rest of the fleet. They passed close in
front of Esashi at dawn on the morning of the 20th, and
landed the troops at the village of Otobé. The troops
at once proceeded to occupy the important position of
Jôgai zan. As soon as the rebels heard that the loyal
forces had disembarked they sent a body of troops, but
the loyal forces fired upon them from their elevated position, while the fleet cannonaded their flank. The rebels
were completely defeated, and retiring to the other side
of the Tsuchiba river, kept up the fight. On this the
fleet turned round and closed in upon Esashi, to the as-
tonishment of the rebels troops at that place and at the

Tsuchiba river, who finally fled to the castle of Matsumaë. The loyal troops then advanced and took possession of Esashi.

On the 22nd the loyal army separated into two divisions in order to attack Matsumaë. One advanced from the Esashi side, the other from the village of Udzura. At this moment the rebels made a violent onset, with loud shouts, hoping to recover Esashi. The loyal army encountered them in fight, but the rebel troops were so ferocious as to come to close quarters with fixed bayonets, and it had to fall back, abandoning its cannon and muskets, and leaving a considerable number of dead on the field. But the other division which had advanced to Kikonai and Futamata inflicted a severe defeat on the rebels.

On the 24th the loyal troops 'with all the men gagged,' took advantage of the morning mist to surprise the rebel quarters at Kikonai and Futamata a second time. The rebels were lying concealed among the hills, and poured in such a hot fire that the loyal troops suffered greatly and were unable to advance. A great battle ensued at Kikonai in which they were finally defeated with great loss.

At this moment five hundred runaway troops from Sendai joined the rebels, who were considerably strengthened by this reinforcement, and the rebel commanders at the castle of Matsumaë, on hearing of the victories at Kikonai and Futamata, determined to make an attack on Esashi with their whole force. At dusk on the 27th they arrived at the village of Kiyobé, on which the Kasuga approached the shore, and opened fire on their flank. The land forces also advanced, and in conjunction with the fleet inflicted a severe defeat on the rebels, killing a great number of their officers. The survivors all fled to Matsumaë.

At daybreak on the 28th the loyal army, both marine

and terrestrial, made a combined attack on Matsumaë. The rebels had occupied the battery at Orido on the highroad, and in defending it their sharpshooters brought down several tens of loyal soldiers, preventing the force from advancing. At the same moment some other loyal troops had proceeded along the hill path, and they also were met by another detachment of rebels ; but by fighting fiercely and advancing with determination they routed them, and came out into the highroad on the other side of Orido, thus getting the enemy between two fires. The fleet had already approached the castle of Matsumaë, and was engaged in bombarding castle, batteries and town. The rebels became so short of cannon-balls that they had to defend themselves with 18-pounder guns loaded with 12-pound shot, and these also came to an end at last. The loyal army, both marine and terrestrial, persisted in the attack, until they completely routed the rebels, who at dusk fled to Fukushima. In this way the castle of Matsumaë was taken by the loyal army, while the rebels continued to hold Fukushima, Shiriuchi and Kikonai.

At six o'clock on the morning of the 30th the loyal troops profited by a dense fog to surprise the rebel quarters at Kikonai. Great confusion ensued among them, which rendered their defeat more easy ; but at this moment the rebels who were at Shiriuchi, hearing of the defeat at Kikonai, suddenly appeared in the rear and fell upon the loyal troops. This revived the courage of the rebels, who returned to the encounter, and the loyal troops, completely caught between two assailants from opposite sides, were defeated and put to flight. The rebels then re-occupied Kikonai.

At eight o'clock on the morning of the 5th June another division attacked Futamata, but the rebels made a stout resistance, and nothing could dislodge them. Fresh men constantly came forward to the fight, and the discharge of artillery re-echoed far and wide. When evening came on the result was still undecided, and both parties withdrew their troops.

At daybreak on the 4th June, the ironclad, the Kasuga, Chôyô, Yôshun, and Teibô, five vessels in all, advanced upon Hakodaté, while the rebels put the Kuaiten, Banrin and Chioda in motion to oppose them, and an engagement cusued in which the opposing squadrons were separated sometimes by 5 *chô* (600 yards), sometimes by 10 *chô* (1,200 yards). The sea appeared to boil over. At noon the fleet withdrew for a while, and shortly afterwards advanced again. The runaway vessels, knowing that they were no match for the loyal fleet, called in the aid of the battery at Benten, and having ascertained the range of the guns in the battery, made a pretended retreat to the centre of the harbour in order to draw on the loyal vessels. When the latter followed the fugitives with yells, the shot from the battery fell right in amongst them, destroying the bridge and battery of the *Chôyô*, and penetrating her side. This did not dishearten the fleet, which continued to advance close, but the increasing intensity of the fire from the battery and want of knowledge of the depth of water prevented it from going far in, and it finally drew off.

The fight which took place at Futamata on the same day was indecisive. The rebel soldiers fired about a thousand rounds from their muskets, which became in consequence too hot to hold, and they were obliged to provide themselves with buckets of water, in which they cooled their weapons at intervals. On the following day several hundred of them made a charge right over the fort, and drove the loyal forces a hundred paces to the rear. Komai Masagorô, a military inspector, saw this from an elevated spot, and filled with impetuous ardour, rushed down straightway at the head of forty or fifty men, trampling the enemy down. This revived the courage of the loyal troops, who returned to the fight and attacked the rebels vigorously, forcing them to retreat and hold their forts. The number of killed and wounded on both sides in this action exceeded four hundred, and the military inspector Komai met his death from a random bullet fired by one of the rebels.

At daybreak on the 9th June the loyal forces, both marine and terrestrial, advanced in concert upon Yaburai. The land army advanced in two divisions, and was encountered by Ôtori Keiské at the head of 500 men. At the same time a detachment of loyal troops began to climb a steep hill at the side of the road, with the intention of attacking the rebel left wing, but were observed and fired upon from a breastwork which the rebels had constructed half-way up the ascent. Many of them were killed, and they had to take another route. Shortly afterwards the whole loyal army, full of enthusiasm, advanced with determination, and succeeded in routing the rebels, while the iron-clad and other ships, approaching the shore, opened fire on the rebel flank. The 100-pounder guns of the iron-clad bombarded the battery without intermission, and destroyed the guns mounted therein. Completely crushed and dispersed, the rebel army abandoned its positions, and fled to the fort of Kaméda and town of Hakodaté, where the fugitives reassembled. Its loss in officers was very great. Upon this the loyal army advanced, and captured the fort, and arrived soon after at Arikawa.

On the 11th June the loyal army advanced to Namaëhama and the village of Ôno. During the night the rebels surprised their camp at Namaëhama, defeated them and forced them back on Oiwaké. During the following night the rebels attacked the camp at Ôno, and retired again; the loyal troops had a hard fight of it, and lost an extraordinary number of killed and wounded.

At daybreak on the 13th the fleet again moved up to the harbour of Hakodaté, where it was encountered by the Knaiten, Banriu and Chioda, which in conjunction with the fort kept up such an incessant fire as caused the sea to rock. A shot from the Kasuga hit the Banrin in her engines, while those of the ironclad killed several tens of men in the fort. The rebel fire slackened suddenly, but the fleet judged it expedient to retire, as the evening was closing in.

At dawn on the 14th, as the iron-clad and other vessels of the fleet were lying scattered in the neighbourhood of Hakodaté, a runaway vessel came forth, and steered straight for the iron-clad and the Chôyô. On perceiving the enemy the ships opened fire, but he continued to advance slowly without returning it, and charged down upon the iron-clad. Recollecting the disaster which had nearly occurred at the port of Miyako, the iron-clad tried to avoid the shock. The Chôyô continued to fire vigorously at the runaway vessel's side, but still she abstained from returning the fire, and passing between the iron-clad and the Chôyô, departed. The two vessels were much puzzled, but on approaching near enough to look, found that she had not a man on board, and that her engines were completely destroyed. They consequently took possession of her, to the great amusement of the rebels, who said: "This is what may be called dead Shokatsu putting living Chindatsu to flight.[70].'" The fact was that the Chioda had gone ashore close to Benten, having lost her way during the night. The captain, one Morimoto, in despair, at once smashed the machinery and broke in the touch-holes of the guns, and then landed in one of the boats. Enomoto and the others censured him for his precipitate action, which was so prejudicial to the cause, and degraded him to the rank of common seaman, but an officer named Ichikawa was so ashamed of the affair that he committed suicide by way of apology to the rest. When the tide turned, the Chioda began to float, and was carried out by the current.

---

(70) An illustration from Chinese history, vide Jiuhasshiriaku, vol. III. p. 80.

On the 18th the fleet weighed from Arikawa and stood over to the harbour of Hakodaté. The rebels had placed the Banriu, which was incapable of steaming, close to the fort, and converted her into a floating battery. The Knaiten was the only vessel which they were able to oppose to the fleet, and a 300-pounder shot which the iron-clad immediately discharged killed several tens of rebel troops, and smashed the excentric, an important part of her machinery, thus rendering her also unable to move. The rebels ran her on to a shoal, and converted her into a floating battery. Some of the shot fired from her struck the bows of the Kasuga and killed several of the loyal troops, after which the fleet retired. On this day the fleet came so close to the runaway vessels that the latter were able to defend themselves with small arms. The fleet might certainly have destroyed the rebel nest with the expenditure of a little time, but it was prevented from following up the attack to its result by ignorance of the depth of water.

On the 17th the loyal army encamped at the villages of Nanaë and Ôkawa, and during the night the rebel leader Furuya made a sortie from the fort at Kaméda at the head of 300 men. It happened to be very rainy and windy; the loyal troops had gone to sleep with less precaution than usual, and the rebels took advantage of this circumstance to attack the camp. A great commotion ensued, and the whole camp arose with speed to engage the enemy, but the night was so dark that no man could see a foot before him. Some of the troops shot down their own comrades by mistake, and the rebels departed after trampling them flat. During the same night a rebel soldier, named Ôkawa, came to the village of Nanaë with several hundred men, and profiting by the darkness to set fire to the camp made an attack; but the loyal troops repulsed him after some hard fighting.

On the 18th Ôtori Keiské came again to Nanaë at the

head of 800 men, but the loyal troops had previously placed men in ambush at Ôkawa and Okagawa, who upon seeing the rebels approach at once opened fire, and put them to flight. The loyal troops pursued them and retreated again at nightfall.

The whole of the loyal forces, both marine and terrestrial, now advanced on Hakodaté. On the morning of the 20th the Kasuga and Yôshun arrived early at the back of the town, while the land forces having been brought up to the village of Samugawa in the Mannen maru and in a flotilla of boats, were placed in ambush among the hills. Soon after the ironclad, the Chôyô and the Teibô closed up to the front of the town. The Banriu had been repaired by this time and the rebels launched her at the fleet, supporting her with the fire of the floating battery Kuaiten and the forts on shore. At this moment the land troops which had been concealed amongst the hills suddenly charged the rebels, broke their line and put them to flight. The Kasuga also advanced to the front and joined the ironclads and her consorts in an unintermitting attack upon the forts and the Banriu, almost capturing the latter. But the rebel commander Matsuoka Hankichi defended himself well, and manœuvred his ship with the greatest swiftness and ease. He ordered a gunner named Nagakura to discharge the 'Napoleon' guns, and the shells struck the powder room of the Chôyo. Black smoke sprang into the air, the roar re-echoed for ten *ri*, and the ship suddenly sank. The rebel troops clapped their hands and shouted repeatedly 'delightful,' while the fleet advanced to save the dead and drowning. Encouraged by the occurrence the rebels returned to the fight, and routing the loyal troops, drove them back to Namaë-hama, under a cross fire from the Banrin. As soon as the ironclad and the Kasuga beheld this, they closed at once upon the Banrin, and poured in so hot a fire as nearly to blow her to pieces. Shrinking from the combat, in which she was no longer able to defend herself, she took to flight and retreated under the fort. The crew then threw her guns into the sea, destroyed the engines, set fire to her and to the Kaiten, and landed. In this manner the rebels lost all their war-vessels, and the loyal land forces being no longer afraid of being taken in the rear, advanced again in a heroic and determined manner to charge the rebels. They slew the rebel leader Hijikata Saizô and forty or fifty more, and the defeated rebels fled to the forts of Kaméda and to the batteries at Chiyoöka and Benten, leaving the loyal army in possession of the town of Hakodaté. The fighting on this day was very fierce, for both the loyal and rebel armies were desperate; it lasted from six o'clock in the morning until six o'clock in the evening.

On the 21st the fleet advanced to attack the fort at Kaméda, and the ironclad shelled it from a distance of thirty *chô* (3,600 yds.) without hitting it, but after the captain had measured the range every shot told. A great part of the breast-work was knocked to pieces and many of the rebels were killed, while the survivors were much discouraged.

On the 22nd, a loyal soldier named Nagayama went to the battery at Benten and suggested to the rebel troops the advisability of surrendering. Many of them wished to do so, but some held an opposite opinion and opposed the idea. Nagayama went again to the rebel camp and saw Enomoto, to whom he pointed out clearly the advantage of submission and the injury which persistence in treason would entail on them. Enomoto was fully alive to the justice of his reasoning, but was afraid of acting contrary to the inclination of his followers; he therefore merely assented vaguely, and thanked Nagayama for the interest he had taken in them. Nevertheless a great number of rebel soldiers deserted secretly, and came to surrender themselves.

On the 25th the loyal army sent a different messenger to Chiyoöka to talk the rebels over, but instead of obeying the order, they insulted the bearer of it. This excited the anger of the loyal army, which thereupon advanced in three bodies from Nanaë-hama and Kikiôno. Captain Kijima Raizô, attacking Chiyoöka at the head of his troops, was hit in the right leg by a rebel bullet, but disregarding his wound, he continued to cheer on his men. Taruzawa, Kamiyama, Mori, Sudô, Iwami, Shirako and others broke in the gates or jumped over the ditch. The rebel general Nakajima Saburoské, a valiant man with his two sons Tsunétarô and Fusajirô, and Shibata, Asai, Kondô, Fukunishi and others ascended the breastwork and resisted the attack. Taruzawa distinguished himself by engaging Nakajima; seven times they separated and seven times they met again, until after receiving more than ten wounds and being covered with his own blood, he succeeded in laying Nakajima low; but his own life was the price of his victory. During this interval the rest of the loyal troops slew Nakajima's two sons, Shibata and the rest, and having defeated the rebel army completely, captured their encampment.

Shortly before this, when the rebel army was so severely defeated, Enomoto Kamajirô sent a present to the loyal army consisting of two volumes of 'The complete digest of the maritime laws of all nations,' which he had formerly studied when in Holland. The Military Counsellors addressed a letter to Enomoto, in which they said: " We " thank you for presenting us with two volumes the like " of which are not to be found in Japan, out of regret " that they should become the property of the crows. " Your generous feeling lays us under a great obligation. " Some day or other we will cause a translation of them " to be published throughout the empire, and we hope you " will have no cause to regret this act." They also sent five tubs of *saké*, and said by way of thanks, " a slight con- " solation offered to the officers and *samurai* for their " fatigues."

On the 26th Tajima Keizô, a loyal soldier, persuaded Enomoto and his companions to surrender, and on the following day the rebel leaders, that is to say, Enomoto Kamajirô, Matsudaira Tarô, Arai Ikunoské and Ôtori Keiské actually gave themselves up at the loyal camp, in order that they might suffer punishment in place of the many. Their surrender was followed by that of Nagai Gemba, Matsuoka Hankichi, Sôma Kaznyé and others. When the rebel army made up its mind to surrender, the commanders had sent a messenger to Mororau with orders for the evacuation of that place, and the troops which had been stationed there now came in and surrendered. All the prisoners were subsequently sent to Yedo.

In this campaign the rebels had the advantage of possessing in their naval force men well acquainted with their profession, and the place they had to defend was naturally strong from its position. These two things caused the heavy losses suffered by the loyal army, but on the other hand the iron-clad, which advanced without being at all affected by the shots which struck her, was a source of great annoyance to the rebels.

When Enomoto and his companions first absconded from Shinagawa three Frenchmen shared their flight, in order to assist them in their operations, but when the failure of the operations became evident, Enomoto talked them over and sent them back to Tôkiô. The Government consequently informed the French representative that it could not allow these persons to remain in the country. The French representative punished them, and when Hakodaté was taken, sent them back to their native land. This was done because they had violated the neutrality.

During the same month the ringleaders belonging to the Aidzu and other clans underwent the penalty of the law. Shortly afterwards a *Shôkonsha* (Shrine for welcoming spirits) was erected on Kudanzaka in Banchô (at Yedo) for the celebration of rites in honour of those who fell fighting on the 3rd day of the 1st month (Jan. 27, 1868 at the battle of Fushimi) the 15th of the 5th month (July 4, 1868 at Uyeno in Yedo) and the 23rd of the 9th month (Nov. 7 1868, before Wakamatsu), on account of the great importance of the battle of Fushimi, the fight at Uyeno and the surrender of Aidzu. A telegraph was erected from Tôkiô to Yokohama to facilitate the communication of business.

In the 6th month (July 20—August 17) an Imperial proclamation was issued by which rewards were granted for the military services performed since 1867 and 1868. Pensions and sums of money were granted to the Hiôbukiô no Miya (Ninnaji no Miya) the Dazai no Sotsu Miya (Arisugawa no Miya), to Kujô Sadaijin, Sawa Sammi and twenty-one Court nobles (*kugé*), to the houses of Shimadzu and Môri and the chiefs of eighty-eight other clans, to Saigô Kichinoské, Ômura Masujirô and more than a hundred other individuals. Shortly afterward the offices of Sadaijin, Udaijin, Dainagou and Sangi were created, and the names of all other offices under Government were reformed. As official titles had been little more than empty appellations since the chronological period called *Daihô* (701-703) it was determined that henceforward the titles should correspond to the reality.

In the spring of this year the clans of Satsuma, Chôshiu, Tosa and Hizen addressed a memorial to the Throne, in which it was argued that the *daimiôs*' fiefs ought not to be looked upon as private property, and leave was asked to restore the registers of the clans to the Sovereign. The other clans followed the example. The Court, however, declined to decide on its own authority, and only accorded its consent after consulting the general opinion. Shortly afterwards the designations of Court nobles (*kugé*) and territorial princes (*shokô*, more commonly called *daimiô*) were abolished and replaced by that of noble families (*kuazoku*). A new constitution was framed by which the three forms of administration called city (*Fu*), clan (*Han*) and district (*Ken*) were combined in one whole, and the former lords of the clans were temporarily appointed Governor of clans (*Chihanji*), the feudal system being thus completely changed. From this moment the governmental power was concentrated in the family of the sovereign, and the Empire was grateful for universal peace.

The End.

www.ingramcontent.com/pod-product-compliance
Lightning Source LLC
Chambersburg PA
CBHW030332170426
43202CB00010B/1099